Preaching to Every Pew

Preaching to Every Pew
Cross-Cultural Strategies

James R. Nieman and Thomas G. Rogers

Fortress Press
Minneapolis

PREACHING TO EVERY PEW
Cross-Cultural Strategies

Cover image: Copyright © 2001 Photodisc. Used by permission.
Cover design: David Meyer
Book design: Ann Delgehausen

Library of Congress Cataloging in Publication Data
Nieman, James R.
  Preaching to every pew : cross-cultural strategies / James R. Nieman, Thomas G. Rogers.
      p. cm.
  Includes bibliographical references (p.).
  ISBN: 0-8006-3243-5 (alk. paper)
    1. Preaching. 2. Christianity and culture. I. Rogers, Thomas G., 1952–
II. Title.

BV4235.S6 N54 2001
251—dc21   2001040678

The paper used in this publication meets the minimum requirements of American National Standard for Information Sciences—Permanence of Paper for Printed Library Materials, ANSI Z329.48-1984.

Manufactured in the U.S.A.   AF 1-3243
05   04   03   02   01   1   2   3   4   5   6   7   8   9   10

Contents

Preface

We can see it everywhere. From broad immigration patterns to local demographic shifts all the way to marriage and adoption within individual families, we can see the massive cultural diversity in American society. Nor are our churches untouched by it. This diversity reaches even into the soul of worship whenever preachers speak to those whose cultural realities are profoundly different from their own. How can we reach this wide range of hearers on any given Sunday through a single sermon? How can we speak an authentic word amid people whose unique experiences and values bring unfamiliar expectations of the preacher? How can we attune our preaching for a particular setting without distorting the gospel we announce? This book explores these various complications to preaching in our culturally diverse society and offers concrete strategies for addressing an immense and growing challenge.

We began this project as teachers seeking a text that did not yet exist. Our seminary students and the pastors we met in continuing education events were facing situations of enormous cultural diversity yet were unclear about how to reach beyond their own cultural backgrounds in their preaching. When they asked for advice about what to do, we could offer only a few scattered resources. Compelled by their requests, therefore, we began this project as teachers seeking a text. Before long, however, we became the learners. Knowing the limits of our own insights and perspectives, we did what any teacher might do: we looked for others to teach us.

The wealth of reflections and advice offered through this book come from actual preachers in real congregations. Each of these experienced preachers is familiar with distinctive cross-cultural challenges, and we simply asked them to comment upon how this has affected and continues to reshape their preaching. By reading portions of these extensive interviews, you will encounter these preachers in their own words. Their concrete remarks are enhanced along the way by our own insights as the authors, who each teach preaching at the seminary level and have our own practical experiences with preaching in culturally diverse settings. The result is neither a simplistic "how to" of techniques nor a "one size fits all" approach to preaching in the midst of cultural diversity. Instead, we invite you to reflect deeply with a rich variety of colleagues about the realities of cross-cultural preaching and then draw conclusions appropriate for your own setting.

Our mutual reflection begins in chapter 1 by presenting the theological and analytical approach that unfolds throughout the remainder of the book. After introducing some background to the specific multicultural situation we face today, we present a theological image by which we wish to understand the culturally diverse recipients of our preaching. We also introduce an analytical device for focusing on specific aspects of culture present in any setting (which we refer to as "frames"), as well as a sketch of our research method. The actual results of the interviews are contained in chapters 2 through 5, each of which adopts the perspective of a particular cultural frame. These four chapters use a similar structure of exploring the framing issue, naming the group characteristics of that frame that bear upon preaching, and then giving specific preaching strategies. Finally, chapter 6 returns to a broader scope to consider how we are thinking differently about proclamation due to this closer attention to cultural diversity. We draw together several new perspectives on both the role of the preacher and the task of preaching and then return to a central theological image from the outset of the book.

For the patient instruction of those we interviewed or who otherwise contributed to the substance of this book, we are deeply grateful. Those persons include Daniel Anderson-Little, Linda Anderson-Little, Gaylon Barker, Brad Beckmann, Rob Begate, Susan Birkelo, Stacy Boorn, Ray Breton, Martin Brokenleg, Rigoberto Caloca-Rivas, Jean Che, James Chuck, Steve Churchill, Jude Ciciliano, Lars Clausen, Jeff Clayton, David Cleeland, Steve Dahl, Susan Wolfe Devol, Ed DoCompo, Rueben Dominguez, Gerry Drino, Don Drummond, Alex Garcia-Rivera, Josh Garvin, Ron Gwikow, Donald Gilmore, Francisco J. Goitia-Padilla, Douglas Groll, Bob Haigwood, Duane Hanson, Tim Hart-Andersen, Don Headley, Marlene Whiterabbit Helgemo, Pablo Hemanez, Sam Hernandez, Steve Herzberg, Jim Hodner, Bo Holland, Mark Houglum, Gary Johnson, Marina Lachecki, Ted Lam, Warren Lee, Ian McKenzie, Ross Merkel, Charles Miller, Ron Moore, Jack Moriarity, Osvaldo Mottesi, Minh-Hanh Nguyen, Quang Minh Nguyen, Maurice Nutt, Tim Perkins, Gary Peterson, Larry C. Peterson, Larry M. Peterson, Jim Pladsom, JoAnn Post, Jane Ralph, Jose Rodriguez, Bill Ruth, Marv Sandness, Paul Schultz, Pedro Suarez, Hei Hachiro Takarabe, Ann Tiemeyer, Alicia Vargas, Lydia Villanueva, Dave Wangaard, Randall Wilburn, William Wrieden, and Phyllis Zilhart. In addition, we acknowledge Peter Rehwalt for his help in transcribing most of the interviews and conducting several of them in conjunction with a Newhall Fellowship. For various reasons including privacy, this list does not include all those we consulted. Let it stand, however, as a sign of thanks and admiration for the remarkable work of all those who embrace the cross-cultural challenge of preaching, without whose help this book would not be possible. For any errors introduced into their wisdom, we apologize and take full responsibility.

We dedicate this book to the pastors and students whose questions urged us onward to write it and for whom it is intended.

1. And Who Is My Neighbor?

At heart, this book concerns a challenge as dramatic as any ever faced in the American pulpit. In another way, however, it presents a reality as old as the church itself and as widespread as its furthest reaches. That challenge is how to speak beyond one's own cultural home and proclaim the gospel across the boundaries of ethnicity, class, and religious difference. Of course, this is nothing other than the missionary drive of the church since its very beginnings. Had not the first believers been effective at preaching amid those who were different from themselves, the church would not have endured beyond that first generation. Moreover, had not every subsequent generation of believers taken up that same challenge anew in its own place and time, then the gospel itself would be but a faint voice on the horizon of many competing religious claims.

The difference today is that this challenge is not being faced by a few preachers out in some remote mission field. Instead, more and more American preachers are finding themselves in congregations and communities here at home already loaded with enormous cultural diversity. What is more, their training in preaching, whether in the classroom or following the example of a mentor, has often left them ill prepared to take up this challenge in new and creative ways. Why this situation has emerged distinctively in our society will be a subject for later in this chapter. What we can do to address this challenge in our own generation will be our primary focus for the remainder of this book.

Before all that, however, let us briefly consider a few stories of preachers facing the challenge we have mentioned. Each of these incidents portrays actual situations, although the identifying features have been changed. Perhaps in them you will find a mirror of your own setting or something not too far around the corner.

1

Unmarked Intersections

First Christian Church was at a crossroads in more ways than one. As a matter of location, it stood at the corner of Eleventh and Lamar, the latter being a main north-south artery in this major Southeastern city. But this location wasn't merely geographic, for Lamar was also a symbolic dividing line. To its east were the prominent homes and apartments of The Promenade, a century-old neighborhood now being revitalized. To the west of Lamar, however, were the crumbling facades of a once vibrant business district whose owners had long since fled.

It was this very location that gave First Christian its split personality. Many members were of the "gray flannel" variety, either recent residents of The Promenade or longer-standing members who drove in from the suburbs. But on the other hand, folks from the west side of Lamar were also making their presence felt. The church ran a soup kitchen that fed some two hundred persons from that neighborhood each day. When a few of these same people bravely showed up on Sunday morning as well, it was just what Pastor Fred Monroe had hoped.

Not everyone shared his enthusiasm, however. First, the ushers needed to be reminded that fashion was not a qualification for being seated. Next were the scattered efforts to close the soup kitchen as a hazard to health and safety. The clincher then came at the April evangelism committee meeting when Fred led an hour-long walk through the neighborhood, including *both* sides of Lamar. They saw it all: the neat homes and lawns to the east, and the filth and neglect to the west. In both cases, they saw people simply trying to make life work, in good settings or ill.

None of the contrast, however, evidently made much of an impression on the members of the evangelism committee. At the end of the tour, some remained unclear about why it had been conducted in the first place. Wasn't their job to recruit new members? The committee chair was a bit testier, gesturing in irritation toward the west and blurting out, "They're just not our concern!" Finally, one committee member summed up the mood of the rest when she nodded her head in the direction of The Promenade and wistfully wondered, "How can we attract more of *them*?"

Confused, Fred wondered just what such "evangelism" meant for First Christian and what commentary that made on his preaching. Perhaps some people could wear blinders or hope for a more tailored crowd, but he couldn't afford that luxury. Each Sunday, as he preached, Fred could sense the chasm separating those seated only a few feet apart, a difference he dare not ignore. If all he had was a solitary sermon to offer them all, then he was left with a truly haunting evangelism question: what message was being heard by such very different people?

The Question

Pastor Karen Marshall joked that she had the best of both worlds: a full-time pastor position at her own church with no formal duties on Sunday mornings! Of course, the reasons for this arrangement left her no less busy on Sundays than other ministers, and in some cases even busier. She was the pastor for a group of Alaskan Natives who had migrated to Anchorage from villages in the far north of the state and yet retained their Presbyterian roots. With few financial resources, however, they didn't own a building; instead, they borrowed space wherever it could be found.

And this was why Karen had her Sunday mornings "free." Her worship services were held at the big downtown Presbyterian church on Sunday *evenings,* when that building was not in use. Most Sunday mornings found her in various local churches, preaching or teaching with a particular emphasis on Native issues. She enjoyed this double exposure to other groups, seeing it as a chance to share her own congregation's special witness to a broader array of Christians. As a result, the added sermons and classes even felt refreshing.

There was one part of this extra ministry, however, that Karen found both burdensome and bemusing, something she had come to label as "The Question." It always happened the same way. When the worship service at which she had been the guest preacher ended, she would greet people at the door and receive their many generous remarks about her preaching. Then it came: "The Question," offered in the most innocent fashion imaginable. "Pastor, don't you have to make your sermon a whole lot simpler for those Native people?"

How was she supposed to respond to *that*? She knew from quizzing her questioners over the last five years that they weren't saying something about her preaching already being complex. Most people actually found her lively and accessible. Instead, she began to realize that "The Question" revealed the biases of those who asked it, who were typically white, educated, and well-off. It exposed a perception that some people were mature enough for "solid food" from the pulpit while others were not. It was a question based on privilege.

Perhaps Karen should fire back that any group that could endure the stress of straddling two cultures for five generations was far from simple-minded. The more she thought about it, however, she knew that wasn't the whole story. In fact, Karen's congregation *did* hear sermons differently than others she had met. When she preached from prophetic oracles about the mistreatment of the poor or from Mary's song about the lowly being lifted up, her members didn't hear old, unpleasant words. They heard instead a vivid hope. They heard a message *for them.*

Coming Home

It was the kind of call Jerry Eldredge had hoped to receive. Long ago, he had left his rural Midwestern home for college and then a business career that led him all over the United States. Even so, his Nebraska roots were deep. So when, at the age of fifty-one, he entertained the crazy idea of ending his first career and beginning a new calling as a pastor, Jerry had harbored the secret hope that such service would bring him back home. Indeed it did, although not exactly. Fresh from seminary, his first call in fact returned him to a Nebraska he had never known.

In some ways, Emmanuel Lutheran Church seemed like his childhood parish: a small-sized, slow-moving congregation with modest resources. The town in which it was located, however, was swept up in a torrent of changes no one could have foreseen thirty years earlier. The construction of a beef-processing plant in 1987 had been hailed at the time as the economic salvation of this community of 15,000. When the population swelled by the thousands with an influx of Latino workers and their families, however, the strains on the social fabric were evident everywhere.

Jerry had seen such changes in other places he had lived, and he welcomed the emerging ethnic diversity. He also recognized the tensions and puzzled over how he and the congregation might respond. In his interview with the congregation before accepting the position, he flatly rejected any sort of "head in the sand" response. If Emmanuel were to call him, they would have to be willing to enter the fray and make some choices. The good-hearted members accepted that challenge, but now everyone wondered what to do next, including Jerry.

An astute observer, Jerry spent a good bit of his first six months in Jefferson noticing how other churches had been reaching out to the Latino population. The Roman Catholics started a separate Spanish mass on Sunday afternoons that was only sparsely attended. The Methodists hired a minister from Ecuador, but his urban background set him at a distance from the rural Mexican immigrants. The Pentecostal house churches were the only ones that seemed to flourish, but with no stable leadership they also easily withered, only to sprout anew elsewhere.

So just what was a tradition-bound Danish Lutheran congregation to do? With no money for added staff and no ability of his own in Spanish, Jerry knew a separate ethnic outreach was unfeasible. Was that the only option? Maybe another approach could focus less on a new program in the community and more on what he said from the pulpit. Could his sermons shape how members viewed these newcomers? Could he help Emmanuel see what it might have in *common* with these more recent immigrants? Could he forge a bond, if not for his own generation, perhaps for their *children*?

Unexpected Lessons

When Plymouth Congregational Church first decided to start a preschool program, it did so as a way of reaching out to its neighborhood in suburban King County, Washington. Everyone knew it meant running a bureaucratic maze of permits, certifications, and inspections. A smaller circle of organizers also knew it meant a marketing challenge, assuring the parents of potential enrollees that this new program was high quality and reliable. No one, however, including Pastor Carol Larsen, ever dreamed that such a school meant a challenge, of all things, to *preaching.*

The weekly preschool schedule included an informal chapel service each Wednesday morning. The congregation had actually insisted upon it in order to emphasize that this was an outreach of the church. Parents were well aware of this feature and seemed open to it. Carol was aware of it, too, since it fell to her to organize the worship. She welcomed the challenge of trying to engage this very young audience in song and prayer, and she also hoped to speak to them about the faith, to offer them the gospel in a way that was fitting.

As the enrollments came in, however, the staff and pastor marveled at who would be attending. Although many of the ninety children came from white families within the congregation, fully a third were from Japanese immigrant homes. Ten children were Latino, two more were Hmong, another two Indonesian, and there was even one Croatian. Of course, a simple trip to the grocery store revealed the same multicultural flavor of the area. What amazed everyone was that this diversity would now be coming *inside* a church that, to this point, was virtually monocultural.

What concerned Carol even more had to do with that part of the enrollment form asking for religious affiliation. Besides the familiar "UCC" or "Protestant" or blank responses, she encountered a wild array of "Buddhist" and "Hindu" and "Muslim," along with Christian groups she didn't immediately recognize. Naturally, she had seen the buildings of these various faiths in the neighborhood and had noted the religious attire of some or how others honored family graves at the local cemetery. Even so, who would have thought such people might now be hearing her preach?

What would it mean to speak of Jesus to children who lacked all background in Christianity? How could she offer an honest witness that neither watered down the scripture nor trampled on the religious traditions of her young listeners? What would these children say to their parents at home about what they had heard from her at preschool? What if their parents actually visited on Sunday morning? Out of the utterly unrelated effort to establish a preschool, Carol's entire approach to preaching was about to receive a new education.

Naturally, each of these incidents is distinctively shaped by the personalities, programs, cultural groups, and regions involved. At the same time, however, there are important similarities that lay the foundation for comparing these very diverse situations, as well as the many others we encountered while preparing this book. First among these similarities is that the cross-cultural challenge to preaching is neither exotic nor rare, but can be found virtually anywhere in our society. Whether urban or rural, large church or small, on the coasts or in the heartland, congregations and their leaders are realizing that ethnic, class, and religious diversity are as close as next door. Not only is such variety found everywhere, its arrival may not be very recent, either. Pastors like Fred Monroe ("Unmarked Intersections") and Carol Larsen ("Unexpected Lessons") did not stumble upon recent neighborhood changes, but were coming to grips with matters of long duration.

A second important similarity is that the origins of this challenge to preaching most often derive from forces *outside* the pulpit. In the course of our research, we really never found a case where the sermons reached across cultural boundaries simply because the preacher thought that this would be an innately good idea! Instead, preachers were responding to some other reality that had subsequent implications for the pulpit. Sometimes that "other reality" is a change in the program of the congregation, as with Fred Monroe's soup kitchen or Carol Larsen's preschool. Rather than new programs, perhaps a church or its leaders begins to attend more deeply to ideas like "evangelism" or "hospitality," which then leads to changes in education, budget, worship, and (not surprisingly) preaching.

Very often, however, the kinds of shifts that prompt a challenge to preaching are the result of forces far beyond the congregation itself. When, for example, Jerry Eldredge arrived in Jefferson ("Coming Home"), he faced ethnic tensions arising from industrial and employment decisions that had no real link to Emmanuel Lutheran itself. Likewise, the unusual shape of Karen Marshall's Sunday schedule ("The Question"), a schedule that allowed her to see how different her various listeners were, had its real source in the urban relocation of rural Alaskan Natives that long predated her own congregation.

A third similarity among these stories and the many others we heard is the way the cross-cultural challenge to preaching is being successfully addressed. Although there are only hints of what finally happened in the stories above, it should be fairly clear that no single, magic solution works for all of them. This is an exceptionally important point to absorb here at the outset of this book. If you seek easily acquired gimmicks and techniques to aid your preaching, you should know right away that those we interviewed have no such quick fixes to offer. In most cases, we met pastors who simply had to immerse themselves in the very hard work of changing the way they preached from the ground up. They spent a great deal of time learning about a culture that was unfamiliar and then building trust with that group. They also remained open to change and critique, realizing that they were always "in process" in learning to preach across cultural boundaries.

So what was the specific outcome of all that work? Certainly, preachers like Carol Larsen and Fred Monroe ended up actively trying to address multiple hearers within the same congregation. For folks like Jerry Eldredge, however, the challenge became a less flashy one: how to speak in a new way to the same old hearers, with the long-term aim of affecting the next generation. In addition, the attempts at Latino ministry in Jefferson reveal that even the best efforts at cross-cultural preaching will not adapt to every situation! Finally, for preachers like Karen Marshall (and Fred Eldredge, too) all that work had only an indirect impact upon preaching, leading instead to more substantial changes in teaching, stewardship, and so forth. Consequently, the chapters to come sometimes will speak more about the context that supports preaching than about offering advice about preaching itself.

The final similarity among these stories is the impetus to move from a cross-cultural challenge to preaching toward finally addressing it. In short, it all begins with *recognition*. As with Karen Marshall, we must recognize that there are real differences in how people hear preaching, based on their experiences and stations in life. As with Fred Monroe, we must recognize that other cultural groups cannot hear us until we learn more about those differences and adjust our language appropriately. As with Carol Larsen, we must recognize that denial, watered-down content, or rank insensitivity are inappropriate strategies for communicating with those whose worldview differs from our own. As with Jerry Eldredge, we must recognize that it is not impossible to take up this cross-cultural challenge. Others have addressed it, and this book lays out their wisdom.

So let this be an invitation to the sort of recognition we have sketched so far, a recognition that can move us from challenge to action. In this regard, the term *recognition* (from the Latin *re + cogniscere*, literally "to know again") has three senses: honor, familiarity, and insight. As a kind of honor, we recognize others by respecting their intrinsic dignity. As a kind of familiarity, we recognize others through the growing appreciation we develop for them over time. As a kind of insight, recognition of others leads to a reappraisal of ourselves and a rethinking of our deepest commitments. In the pages ahead, we invite you into this full range of "recognition" as you ponder the challenge of how to preach among those different from yourself.

As a starting-point for that task, it will be fruitful to recognize just what sort of cross-cultural situation exists in our society. For both preachers and congregations, what has happened to lay this challenge before us today?

Multicultural America

It might be expected at this point to offer a dizzying array of demographic data about the cultural diversity facing our society in the coming century. Newspaper headlines like "Iowa's Hispanics to Double in Twenty Years" and Census Bureau reports entitled "Black Population Grows in Younger Groups" are familiar enough and reinforce a subtle form of fear-mongering about the future. The challenge we mean to address in these pages, however, is not about tomorrow. It is a reality for congregations today. The faithful response to this, regardless of the cultural background of a congregation, is not some additional fear-driven reinforcement of already narrow, religious enclaves. Instead, congregations and leaders must address the contexts in which they *already* find themselves as part of Christ's mission to the whole world. If we can begin there, then it actually matters far less what sort of changes lay *ahead* than what are the origins of our *present* situation. To understand that, we must first notice what we have long chosen to ignore and then name one particular event that has rearranged our social landscape.

What we have long chosen to ignore is that America already has a history as a culturally diverse society. Unfortunately, much of that history can only be viewed negatively through the repression of various peoples. Cultural diversity was reflected in the founding documents of this nation when Native Americans were denied citizenship and African Americans received only partial enumeration and no franchise. Cultural diversity was also present in the grim routes of immigration, much of it voluntary (Europeans), some of it only questionably so (Chinese and Mexican), and an important part of it not at all by choice (again, African Americans). Within our own time, the many policies restricting contact between some cultural groups (through racial segregation) or limiting the full citizenship of others (through literacy tests for voting) further testify to the fact that America has always been a multicultural society. When economic class is understood as a cultural category (as we shall portray it), yet another form of diversity weaves its way through American life. The problem for us today, however, is not this long history of cultural diversity itself, but that we have chosen to fear rather than welcome it.

Sadly, the church has participated in reinforcing this refusal. When Martin Luther King Jr. claimed that Sunday morning was the most segregated time of the week, he simply exposed the church's role in legitimating and perpetuating bigotry and intercultural hatred. Repeatedly in our research for this book, we encountered settings that were not very culturally different from what they had been ten, twenty, or even fifty years before. Why was there so little sense of the challenge of cultural diversity for preaching back then? Regardless of the reason, what has changed more recently and remarkably is that eyes are at last being opened to see the settings in which congregations have long existed.

This also suggests perhaps the greatest single challenge to preaching across cultural boundaries: the openness to or denial of the multicultural reality in which churches are already to be found. This is the reason why we spend so little time here presenting yet more statistics to convince you of what you and others in your community probably already know. At the same time, however, we want to address this challenge now because we believe we stand in a time of hope, when many Christians (some of them even being preachers!) are actually willing to embrace the challenge before them. That is why we take such care later in this opening chapter to present a theological rationale for preaching to those beyond our own cultural home. We want to argue why the church as church (as opposed to, say, a social club or special interest group) has particular reason to care about cultural diversity in the task of preaching.

Even though, as we have already said, so much of America's cultural diversity is really nothing new, there is one recent event that *has* significantly altered the social landscape in which many congregations find themselves. That event was the passage of the Immigration Act of 1965. To understand the dramatic changes brought by that single piece of legislation, we must briefly examine the backdrop of immigration policy up to that time. Since America has so often been portrayed as a nation of immigrants (a claim which, of course, omits the role of Native Americans), it may be surprising to realize that no comprehensive policy on the subject existed until 1921. Prior to that time, piecemeal legislation provided only for the reporting and policing of immigrants. These laws also identified various categories of persons to be excluded on the basis of politics, health, or morality.

The First Quota Act of 1921, however, established a system of "national origins" quotas that remained in tact for the next four and a half decades. In the midst of the Cold War, the Immigration and Nationality Act of 1952 reinforced this system, giving preference to Northern and Western Europeans. Proponents of that Act, mindful of the Nazi regime, were careful not to argue their case on the grounds of racial superiority, but rather on sociological theories of cultural assimilation and balance. Such theories also conveniently preserved historically severe restrictions on Asian immigration. Nonetheless, in a curious twist, the 1952 legislation was largely ineffective. A host of special laws during the rest of the decade admitted various special refugees (especially those escaping communist regimes), thus diminishing the intent of the quota system.

An amendment was needed, which came in the form of the 1965 Immigration Act. Reflecting the spirit of the times, this new Act sought to portray America as a world leader not only in its nondiscriminatory internal policies (like recent civil rights legislation), but also in its openness toward those from other parts of the world. As a result, the 1965 Act completely scrapped the national origins quota system, replacing it with general immigration ceilings that were comparable for both the Eastern and Western Hemispheres. More importantly, the Act made explicit the historic American concern that immigration should reunite families and enrich the labor pool. A new preference system therefore favored close relatives of American citizens and permanent resident aliens, persons with exceptional skills or those in short supply, and political refugees. While such preferences were controversial, few expected any practical changes to result. Europeans, it was thought, would continue to predominate in immigration, since Asians, who at the time amounted to only half of a percent of the American population, would surely have few family ties that could attract relatives from the Eastern Hemisphere. Although immigration is always a touchy labor issue because it might displace native-born workers, the skill and supply restrictions would surely minimize the number of those immigrating for occupational reasons.

The actual outcome, however, was evidently not what anyone expected. Ever since the law was enacted, Asian immigration has steadily increased. While Mexico as a nation accounts for the single largest number of immigrants, the next four most important countries are all Asian (the Philippines, China, Korea, and Vietnam). These changes took place quickly. A simple comparison of the decade just before the Act took effect with the one just afterward shows that immigrants from Asia increased threefold and those from the Americas (again, mostly Mexico) grew around 15percent, while those from Europe dropped by nearly a third. The contrast between the period of the 1952 Act and today is even more startling. In both eras, North American immigrants remained at just over a third of the total. While Europeans represented around half of the immigrants in the 1950s and Asians just under a tenth, however, those proportions today are almost exactly the opposite. Compounding this shift, the raw number of immigrants has vastly increased in the last ten years, partly due to the way undocumented aliens have been classified since 1986 and partly due to temporary efforts to relieve the immigration backlog of the early 1990s. The net result is that a trend of predominantly European immigration that had not wavered since the very founding of the nation has been completely reversed.

These changes, of course, have not gone unnoticed by congregations and leaders. Immigration itself is certainly nothing new, but the shifting patterns since 1965 (which have only been reinforced by later and sometimes controversial legislation) represent a new sort of challenge. Naturally, this means that we recognize today the changing *ethnicity* of our country. As a result of changing ethnicity, we also recognize a range of religious *beliefs* never before encountered as widely on the American scene. In addition, the sheer size of recent immigration means that we recognize the poignant *displacement* of those who live in a land whose worldview is unfamiliar and disorienting. Finally, we recognize, in the economic struggles of these newcomers, the broad *class* issues facing many people in our communities, immigrant and otherwise. All told, congregations and leaders recognize now as never before how America, which has always been multicultural, is experiencing that longstanding reality in ways that have quite new and distinctive contours.

Choosing Our Words Carefully

Even though we may recognize this challenge, why should we care about it? Except for rabid ideologues, this is a genuine question being asked in many congregations (though perhaps only in hushed tones), and it demands a thoughtful response. After all, the foregoing sketch could sound like a largely social and cultural matter best met through civic virtues of fairness and legal mandates for justice. As a result, many Christians have been left to view multicultural America as something "out there" with little or no *theological* import. For some, this has meant a passive resistance. Congregations then gradually become enclaves isolated not only from their own settings but also (and more hauntingly) from realizing the kind of witness this makes to the world. For others, this failure to reflect theologically has meant a passive acceptance. This is no better, for congregations then view the challenge we have described in purely secular terms, just one more moral duty to be faced with stony tolerance, tepid civility, or patronizing charity.

If congregations (let alone preachers) want to live in a posture other than passive resistance or passive acceptance, we must learn to speak anew; for how we name a situation affects how we act toward it. What are the right words to guide the faithful response of those who would be the body of Christ and make that distinctive witness in a multicultural America? We need a language of honest recognition that can, at the same time, offer us direction specifically as *church*. In other words, we need to choose our words with care.

This means searching Christian tradition and the storehouse of scripture for language natural to the faith. Some may find that move woefully parochial, and surely other fields could offer more up-to-date language. Cultural anthropology, whose insights will be important later in this chapter and throughout this book, might naturally be one of these. As a discipline, it would refer to the challenge we have described as an encounter with the "other," those who are irreducibly different from us. Accurate though that may be, it also implies the impassive gaze of an observer and the scrutiny of an object of study (like another culture) for the sake of understanding and even mastery. This is not how our faith views the world.

Words from such disciplines fall short for our purposes because they cannot bear the weight of the mystery that drives our actions as church. Christians are not bid to be neutral about their surroundings. Instead our words are unashamedly value-laden. We are biased people, openly declaring our vested interests with other persons, all of creation, and even God. Perhaps our central bias is the belief that we have been given abundant life, a gift that cannot be contained and longs to be shared. Another bias (and not unrelated) is that we see the shape of such life traced out along the horizon of Christ's final reign. Because we are oriented toward that future, all we do and say until then becomes, at its best, a hope-filled sign pointing toward God's ways for us. For that reason, the very terms Christians have traditionally chosen to depict our relationship with those around us display these twin biases of the gift we bear and the end we anticipate.

One familiar example of this is when we use *sibling* (Paul's use of "brothers/sisters in Christ") or *friend* (Jesus' statement that "you are my friends") to speak of those within the church. These forms of address convey the intimate bonds within the household of faith that are beyond our power (like being born into a family) and yet require our involvement (like choosing a companion). These bonds not only give us a home today, but they also point ahead to that future when we receive a place with others at the table of the Lord. Because of that promised place, all present-day relations within the church have a new character as well, redefined now as siblings and friends.

As rich as this language is, however, it will not work for our present purposes because of its inward focus. To be sure, such names are divinely conferred upon the faithful in every time and place. We are siblings and friends with countless others because God has made us so, not because we consider it a good idea. But the authentic use of such names also presumes mutual relations that at present are lacking. After all, the very challenge we are addressing involves people yet unknown to us, even though in many cases they may be fellow Christians. Under such circumstances, we invite suspicion if we unilaterally label as siblings or friends those with whom we have hitherto had few or no dealings. Moreover, many in this multicultural America will never be part of our household of faith and so would resist our in-house designations. Certainly, siblinghood and friendship are potent terms and may eventually have their place as we faithfully engage the challenge before us. In the meantime, we need a language that can describe our actual situation and direct us outward.

At the other end of the spectrum, our traditions have used names like *stranger* (sometimes called "sojourner") and *people* (sometimes called "Gentiles" or "nations") to speak of those beyond the household of faith. In scripture, strangers were those outsiders who sometimes traveled through or lived within the promised land and thus were the focus of special care and protection. The vulnerability of strangers led the church to use the term in reference to the unresolved status of the believer. We are strangers to the promise until we believe (Ephesians 2:12), after which we become strangers to the world (Hebrews 11:13). But because this name has been used more often about Christians themselves than how they relate to strangers in their midst, it is less helpful for guiding our discussion here.

The term *people* also merits examination. It indicated those with bonds to a social or political reality other than the God of Israel. Because such people followed other ways, they represented a possible threat to Israel's covenant faithfulness and for the same reason were often seen as enemies of God. Clearly, this offers no truly constructive guidance for how congregations could relate cross-culturally today! Moreover, this designation functioned simply as a blanket term for those outside of the covenant. For our purposes, therefore, it flattens out the distinctiveness of the many different cultural groups we daily encounter. Even though scripture holds out a vision of all peoples and nations being drawn to the God of Israel, such a future hope gives little practical direction through our present challenges.

What we need, then, is a language familiar to the church that can chart a course between insider and alien, household and social world, familiarity and rejection. That language, we suggest, is the image of _neighbor_. Its Greek basis alludes to location, "one who is nearby." Moreover, this New Testament usage assumes an underlying Hebrew concept emphasizing relationship. The neighbor is someone we regularly meet, a fellow participant in social encounters. The word thus designates interaction, not just proximity. At the same time, however, the neighbor is clearly not a member of our household. Scripture may call for a particular treatment of the neighbor (to which we will return in a moment), but the difference between relatives and neighbors is not thereby erased. For example, we are not told that the Good Samaritan later became a Judean or joined the household of the victim he aided. He remained, it seems, distinctly Samaritan even in being the quintessential neighbor.

The neighbor, though not a part of our homes, is still a part of our lives and therefore deserves special treatment. That treatment is named at the heart of both testaments in scripture: "Love your neighbor as yourself." It is worth dwelling on this command for a moment in light of the challenge we have been discussing. If the standard for treatment of the neighbor is the measure of love with which we regard ourselves, this raises two fundamental questions. On the one hand, when we lack compassion for those who are culturally different, does that actually signal a deeper self-loathing? At the heart of our difficulties today may be simple failure to trust that we have already been freed from the powers of sin and death to live in openness toward others. And on the other hand, if we would embrace those who are culturally different from ourselves, doesn't that mean doing so with everything at our disposal? Plainly put, to love our cross-cultural neighbor in preaching means sharing the treasure of the gospel we hold so dear. To do any less would be, by contrast, downright unneighborly.

The image of neighbor not only gives a rationale for preaching in cross-cultural settings but also reorients the preaching task itself. Many have noted that, in the parable of the Good Samaritan, Jesus shifts the focus away from the lawyer's request for a definition ("And who is my neighbor?"). More telling than that, Jesus never asks who the _Samaritan_ considered _his_ neighbor to be. Instead, Jesus asks who *proved* (from the Greek *gínomai*, "to become") to be neighbor to the *victim*. In other words, "neighbor" refers to how we act toward fellow human beings, particularly those nearby and in need. It indicates a relationship that says less about the recipient of special treatment than the giver of compassion.

The implication for preaching is important. Preaching that recognizes multicultural realities is, in some important respects, less a matter of the *others* we may hope to reach than of whether *we* make a serious engagement with our particular setting. This is why *any* preaching holds the potential to be deeply cross-cultural, even though it may occur in settings that do not seem terribly diverse or congregations that do not welcome changes in that direction. The issue for *all* preachers is, quite simply: have our words shown us to be a neighbor? This theological rationale also places a serious question before our congregations. If Christ proved to be our ultimate neighbor in his self-emptying love on the cross, what does that imply for those who dare to gather as the body of Christ? The image of the neighbor in a multicultural America thus raises a challenge not only to our preaching, but to our very identity as church.

Cultural Frames

We have recognized the challenge before us in two ways so far. By choosing the theological image of neighbor, we practiced recognition as *honor*, respecting the worth of others. By sketching the origins and scope of multicultural America, we practiced recognition as *familiarity*, appreciating the contours of our situation. It is now time to practice recognition as *insight*, being open to reexamine ourselves and our task. In particular, we need to reconsider the task of preaching itself as it occurs in any particular setting.

No standardized definition of preaching is required for us simply to agree that preaching is an act of communication. Of course, as the discussion just above has already emphasized, we also affirm that preaching requires something more, a particular content with a special aim amid a distinctive gathering. This theological specificity does not, however, diminish the simple and significant fact that preaching involves communication. With word and movement, sound and silence, preaching moves outward from speaker to hearers, sweeping them into a dynamic world of meanings and moods, images and claims. Because preaching is an act of communication, like any such act it is inextricably embedded in culture (a point to which we will return in a moment). If we want new insight into the task of preaching, therefore, we must turn our attention to an understanding of culture.

We need not retrace here the rich and complex development of the term *culture* (although you may wish to consult the Suggested Readings section at the end of this book). Even so, some understandings are quite deeply entrenched and very unhelpful and so should be rejected here at the outset. Contemporary discussions of culture no longer adopt the elitist slant implied in phrases like "high culture" or "being cultured," for culture is not reserved for the privileged or supposedly mature. More pervasive, however, is the unfortunate popular tendency today to equate culture strictly with categories of race or nationality (such as "Black culture" or "Russian culture"), when in fact culture encompasses something much broader than these alone. These distortions aside, we are satisfied here to use a fairly general understanding of culture as *the ways we mark off who we are and give shape to the spaces we inhabit*. Culture is a human construct that includes both our *patterns of meaning* and our *strategies for action*. In fact, anywhere we find human beings, we find cultural work being done (through gatherings, habits, rituals, and more) and cultural traces left behind (in records, artifacts, institutions, and so forth). Therefore, items as different as rules of etiquette, a garbage dump, and a musical performance are equally legitimate expressions of a culture, even though what they display about that culture might be quite varied. Whatever in human society is not just naturally given (and hardly anything is ever left in such a pure state!) is culturally created.

Recent debates about culture add three insights of great importance for the chapters that follow. First, culture is a *process*. Once thought of as a stable force binding people together, culture is now considered to be constantly changing and moving. If culture is a construct, it is also always under construction. Second, culture is a *plural*. Anthropologists no longer speak in the singular about "*the* native," as if each group has a single, monaural culture. Instead, even seemingly homogeneous groups are composed of multiple cultures that are not sealed but porous, influencing one another through cultural borrowing that now spans the globe. Finally, culture is a *paradox*. Much of the twentieth century held to a "pattern" view in which culture represented the shared agreements that regulated life. More recently, however, culture has also been seen as a place of engagement and even struggle. Culture sometimes refers to the consensus people reach, but at other times it points to the contest in which commonly held items are given quite different meanings (as with contemporary American debates about "family values").

We can now return to our earlier claim that communication (of which preaching is one example) is inextricably embedded in culture. All the ways we communicate are, at one level, simply artifacts of culture, widely available tools used to reach out to others. More than just a vestige of culture, however, communication is also a contributor to it, establishing and reinforcing its shared patterns of meaning. Beyond even this, communication is a site of disagreement, a constantly shifting field for testing and contesting alternatives. Like any culture of which it is a part, communication therefore shows itself to be a process, a plural, and a paradox.

Communication is not only embedded in a larger culture but also shaped by it, as studies in cross-cultural communication have long known (see the Suggested

Readings). For example, we can easily and effectively speak with family and friends not simply because we share a common language, but more deeply because we share a range of cultural assumptions gained through regular, close contact. Those assumptions reassure us that an expression or gesture will mean for someone else what we intend it to mean. Remove those shared assumptions and uncertainty in communicating increases correspondingly. When that happens, we rely on other cultural assumptions to reassure us in speaking and listening. These other assumptions are not the particular kind established through close contact over time, but general ones tied to external cues like physical appearance or vocal accent. It is just such reliance that is bound to be faulty. For example, an offbeat remark from a close friend can be interpreted through assumptions about that person's sense of humor or playful language. The same remark from a stranger lacks any such particular assumptions, which can wrongly lead to attributing it to that person's race or gender.

This, however, is a "mindless" way of communicating. It cedes more value to broad cultural categories than they deserve or can bear, and it fails to consider seriously the particular person with whom we wish to communicate. If we desire something other than gross distortions or complete breakdowns, we need a "mindful" procedure that will lead us toward more particular cultural assumptions like those used with close associates. The challenge, of course, is how to move from mindless, general assumptions to mindful, particular ones.

It is that challenge we set out to address in the following chapters. In this limited space, however, we cannot anticipate every conceivable cultural situation, in part because they are so numerous and unique and in part because (as noted earlier) cultures are plural and porous. Moreover, the particular attention needed for effective cross-cultural preaching must finally rest with each specific preacher, who can look deeply into a specific setting in mindful ways. Rather than attempt what only preachers in their own settings can undertake, our task becomes somewhat different. We present several broad perspectives on cross-cultural preaching that have a bearing on the many specific settings in which that task occurs. To do this, we must introduce the idea of "cultural frames."

Such frames are not cultures themselves, but a set of ways to look at any one culture. To view culture through a frame is, as the metaphor suggests, to take a particular point of view on it, one that draws attention toward some features while necessarily minimizing others. A cultural frame limits the focus to a more manageable body of concerns all gathered around the framing issue. Obviously for that same reason, no single frame is enough to make sense of a setting. Instead, frames need to supplement each other and thereby contribute to a more comprehensive picture, like different photographs that display a mountain from many angles.

The cross-cultural challenges facing preaching today are examined in this book through four cultural frames: *ethnicity, class, displacement,* and *beliefs.* None of these four can alone adequately present the cultural contours of a setting, but they instead serve to supplement each other. Of course, there are many other cultural frames we could have chosen, such as gender, generation, education, region (tied to geography or to population density), sexual orientation, or ableness, to name a few. Each of these would surely also offer its own valuable perspective, and some are mentioned in the coming chapters. Two main factors led to selecting the frames we did. First, these four frames appear to be the most potent and pervasive themes emerging from the longstanding multicultural history of this nation, particularly since 1965. Second, each of these frames raises challenges to communication in particular, ones with special bearing for preaching today. When taken together, they symbolize the range of challenges cross-cultural preaching must face and are suggestive of fruitful strategies that could work in many specific settings.

Our aim in this section has been recognition as insight. How, then, does the claim that communication is embedded in culture cause us to rethink our preaching? Fundamentally, it draws us toward a listener-centered view of that task, which has been a dominant theme of the "New Homiletic" that emerged during the 1970s. This interest in hearers is also as ancient as the sixth-century "catalogue of listeners" in the *Pastoral Care* of Gregory the Great. Therefore, attention to culturally embedded communication redirects us to a rich stream of preaching resources that holds special relevance today. In no sense does this mean, however, that preaching may now disregard its substantive work, the effort to convey the scriptural promise of abundant life in vivid terms today. Instead, a listener-centered approach affirms that the effectiveness of preaching is finally measured against whether or not it has been heard. A sermon's substance is surely set in motion by the preacher, but whatever meaning it may attain rests upon its reception by actual hearers. To engage these hearers deeply, especially when we do not share their cultural home, requires that we regard them as the neighbor. Cultural frames offer a practical, disciplined process for understanding that neighbor with seriousness and care.

A Chorus of Voices

We want to be candid in addressing our role as authors of this book. Although we have both had considerable experience with preaching in cross-cultural settings, this hardly makes us experts on the subject, and to claim some general significance because of our particular backgrounds is presumptuous. In addition, we are quite aware of the limitations that our respective social locations place on what we have to say. All of that is why this book draws upon the wider experiences of a diverse group of preachers interviewed about how they preach in cross-cultural settings. What you hold in your hands therefore is not the product of two authors, but a chorus of voices.

Scores of interviews were conducted over a two-year period, some in person and some by telephone. Those we interviewed were actual practitioners who regularly faced the challenge of preaching in cross-cultural settings in their congregations. These persons were identified primarily by reputation. Denominational leaders, fellow preachers, and seminary professors suggested persons known for their effectiveness and mindfulness with this challenge to preaching. At times, an interviewee would also suggest another preacher we should be sure to contact.

One way we refined the possible pool of interviewees was to seek especially those in congregations with a significant presence of Native American, Latino, or Asian participants, or where the participants lived in economic hardship. Naturally, a single congregation would often include two or more of these characteristics. Certainly, no selection of preachers and congregations could adequately reproduce a complete picture of all cultural settings in America today. However, these four groups were chosen because they each offered distinctive cases of at least one (and often all) of the cultural frames of ethnicity, class, displacement, and beliefs. While not statistically comprehensive, these groups are symbolically representative. In addition, we tended not to focus on cultural characteristics already extensively treated in literature about preaching, references to which can be found in any theological library. While it therefore may seem strange not to have targeted African American congregations, for example, there are already many rich resources in that area. Equally important, the presence of African Americans (and others not targeted) was amply reflected through those we did interview and the places they served, even when such groups were not our primary focus.

The resulting group of interviewees included women and men from quite diverse backgrounds. By denomination, we spoke with Roman Catholic, Episcopal, Lutheran, Presbyterian, United Church of Christ, Methodist, and Baptist ministers. By experience level, they ranged from somewhat newer preachers to seasoned veterans, including those who have served in several cross-cultural settings. For obvious reasons, no beginners were included. By ethnicity, they were as complex as the places they served, including Latinos, African Americans, Whites, Native Americans, and Asians. By region, they were spread from west (Alaska to California) to east (New York to Florida) and nine states of the heartland in between. By congregation type, they brought experiences from groups both large and small, found in rural, suburban, and urban settings.

While these diverse preachers were the expert consultants for our research, we also brought a particular expertise of our own. Since we ourselves are experienced preachers and professors who teach preaching, we used our knowledge of homiletics to craft focused interview questions. These questions addressed the broad range of factors relevant to preaching in any cultural setting, which we hoped would elicit from our interviewees their most revealing and helpful insights. An initial set of questions was pretested at the beginning of our research and refined in subsequent interviews, until it became the list included below:

1. Describe the group you currently serve in terms of its cultural diversity and your place in that mix.
2. What do you think we should hear about preaching in this group? (For example, what would an outsider coming in to preach need to know in order to preach as effectively as possible?)
3. What are the goals (or purposes, or nature) of preaching in this group?
4. How do this group's expectations of preaching affect what you do?
5. What background concerns about your listeners (such as justice or socioeconomic issues) affect how you approach the biblical text and craft the sermon?
6. How does this group view the authority of the biblical text, the sermon, and the preacher?
7. How does preaching relate to other forms of strong speech (like story-telling or sayings) or vibrant expression (like music or dance) in this group?
8. What gets in the way of good preaching in this group?
9. What seems to work well in preaching in this group?
10. How does preaching connect with other elements in the worship service?
11. How does this group show its involvement in the preaching event itself (such as call-and-response, movement, silence, or eye contact)?
12. Again, what else do you think we should hear about preaching in this group? (What have we *not* discussed so far, and what other resources are available?)

By sharing these questions here, we intend to offer our first concrete advice to the reader. That advice is to imitate, in your own setting, the approach to research we have described above. Whether through professional acquaintances or by reputation, you could begin to identify those in your area already experienced at this kind of preaching. You can then conduct your own study using these interview questions as a guide, gleaning from expert practitioners the insights most useful in your distinctive situation (which, of course, we cannot anticipate in this book). You will doubtless want to add your own questions to refine the research further, with attention to special themes and challenges in your specific setting. We also recommend that, as often as possible, you ask interviewees for specific examples from their own preaching. Even the most experienced preachers we met were often not terribly reflective about how they went about that task until we engaged them in telling stories drawn from their settings.

reflective

Such interviewing naturally requires flexibility. For instance, we rarely adhered to our list of questions in exactly the order and wording used above. Our most effective interviews in fact unfolded with the rather haphazard flow of a lively conversation and yet managed to address all the topics listed. The real importance of these questions is that, once the interview is underway, they insure that the most important factors in cross-cultural preaching are likely to be covered. Moreover, the process of interviewing helps you to establish relationships and conversation partners that will enrich your preaching over the long run. Perhaps most surprising of all, you will discover that those you interview were once like you, wondering what to do next and who might help. Indeed, they may still be asking those questions today!

The results from these interviews are collected in the next four chapters. Each chapter adopts the perspective of a single cultural frame: ethnicity in chapter 2, class in chapter 3, displacement in chapter 4, and beliefs in chapter 5. Although the arrangement of each chapter is unique, the basic strategy for them all is the same. We organized the interview materials into themes that show how a chapter's cultural frame clarifies key issues for communication, particularly in preaching. Most important, however, we try to let the interviewees speak for themselves. Based on these interviews, we then draw connections and conclusions where appropriate. The final product in each chapter is a mixture of specific advice, useful tools, and general insights. Included in this mix are matters beyond the pulpit, indirect strategies that are often as important as what is said in the sermon itself.

As you read these four chapters, you will note that some topics run through them all. This simply reflects that each cultural frame is something of an abstraction, separated from the rest for purposes of our analysis and discussion. Since these frames overlap in concrete settings, many of the insights about preaching also overlap and echo one another through these four chapters. At the same time, there are some contradictions between the chapters. Advice given by one person may differ wildly from that given by another. This is in part due to the diversity of these preachers' settings, each with its own peculiarities. It is also due to something we mentioned earlier, that there is no single, magic formula to be applied in all situations. Instead, we encountered a tangle of paradoxes and special cases in cross-cultural preaching, just the sort of messiness one might expect in *any* form of ministry.

Related to this, we sometimes present a general insight only to follow it with exceptions to that rule. Moreover, you will likely find yourself disagreeing with what the interviews suggest because of your own knowledge, experience, or situation. This simply underscores that we do not view this book as containing "the answer" to this complex and multidimensional challenge. Instead, our greatest hope is to invite others to address this challenge in their own specific settings, finding the approaches that are appropriate there. What we offer here is a broad gesture in a direction that we hope others will explore, critique, and enrich.

Some of the conclusions in the next four chapters may also seem a little obvious to some readers. This does not invalidate these insights, and in fact we often learned that it was the so-called "obvious" that had been overlooked in failed attempts to engage a specific setting. If we present an insight you have already reached on your own, let that be an assurance that your intuitions correspond with some of the most savvy practitioners we interviewed. Moreover, this demonstrates that one need not be a specialist to engage effectively in cross-cultural preaching. It is more within our grasp than we often realize. As we indicated earlier, preaching across cultures is not something utterly new. It stands in continuity with the great, historic marks of *any* effective preaching.

Having established the "who" and "why" of the challenge before us in chapter 1 (our rationale), and the "what" and "how" from our interviewees in chapters 2 though 5 (our results), we turn finally in chapter 6 to reconsider what we have learned. We present several insights first about the preacher and then about the nature of preaching, using comments from interviews as well as our own interpretive remarks. What is said in that chapter will make little sense, however, without having engaged the interview materials found in chapters 2 through 5. In other words, don't skip to the end of the book! The rich resources of those middle four chapters are the soil in which the insights of chapter 6 are planted. Moreover, we close that final chapter with a theological concern we have raised above, looking once more at what it means to preach to the neighbor. The first and final chapters are therefore the opening and closing curtains to the performance that takes center stage in this book, the chorus of voices to which we now listen.

2. The Frame of Ethnicity

Dan was looking for a challenge, and his second pastorate proved to be just that. Located in a sprawling river city in the upper Midwest, his new congregation had deep roots in an old neighborhood that had already seen several changes in its ethnic makeup. In the late 1960s, therefore, the predominantly white membership was not only committed to that setting, but also to building a multiracial identity in order to remain rooted there. The plan worked. After two decades of steady growth, the congregation could now boast that three-quarters of its members were African American. Once again it truly reflected the ethnic character of the neighborhood.

When Dan began his pastorate, therefore, he thought he had accurately anticipated the setting and what strategies were likely to work there. His plans, however, often fell flat. From the pulpit, for example, he discovered that his listeners were downright resistant to the style of call-and-response preaching that he, as an African American preacher, had known from other black church settings. By the time we met him nearly five years later, Dan's viewpoint was more circumspect:

> When I first came here, I made assumptions that because people are of a certain race or a certain background that therefore this will be the best way for them to hear the gospel, for them to hear God's word for them. But I have learned that just because someone is African American does not mean that preaching patterns that grow more out of the African American tradition will be helpful or appreciated. So it's more a matter of getting to know people. And a lot of it is subtle.

Some readers may regard Dan's observation as painfully obvious. Others may worry that his remarks undercut the very purpose of this book. Why bother with the cross-cultural challenge of preaching if our best intentions still fall short?

A careful review of Dan's words, however, reveals a deeper wisdom that sets the tone for this chapter. First, preachers must confront the *assumptions* they hold about their listeners. Such assumptions are unavoidable and even helpful when they bring an awareness of human diversity. The problem arises, however, when they obstruct an honest engagement with a distinctive people in a new setting. Second, Dan points out that such honest engagement involves *learning* that unfolds over time. Some of that learning means rejecting old biases, while some of it requires intentional study about new groups. Just as important, however, is the key role of human relationships in developing new insights. Finally, Dan underscores the *complexity* of the matter. The challenge to preaching he faced and that we present here involves subtleties and nuances that cannot be reduced to a few catchy slogans or formulas.

Our task in this chapter is to approach that challenge specifically through the cultural frame of *ethnicity*. Ethnicity provides one way of looking at the special concerns affecting cross-cultural preaching. (It is, of course, only one perspective and should be supplemented by the cultural frames used in the chapters that follow.) Ethnicity offers distinctive insights about *group characteristics* and *preaching strategies* in cross-cultural settings, and so these two categories form the broad structure into which our interview responses are gathered. Before we can turn to these, we must become clearer about the meaning of "ethnicity" itself. Why, in particular, do we frame our discussion in terms of ethnicity rather than race?

Race and Ethnicity

Throughout our research, it was striking how often our interviewees and others used the terms *culture, race,* and *ethnicity* as virtual synonyms. To be sure, these ideas are profoundly interrelated in everyday life. For the sake of clarity, therefore, we presented in chapter 1 a deeper view of culture that was more accurate and helpful for our purposes. In the same way, race and ethnicity must now also carefully be distinguished, both to preserve the undeniable significance of the former and to benefit from the broader scope of the latter.

Any contemporary analysis of the term *race* is, however, venturing onto explosive terrain. Such discussions are often quickly accused of masking one or another political agenda. We therefore wish to be clear that our purpose is simply to discern which categories are most useful for cross-cultural analysis of preaching. Although we argue that "ethnicity" is more revealing in this regard, our aim is not to de-racialize the preaching context or deny the racism that still plagues our society. Instead, we think the category of race becomes most potent for cross-cultural preaching when lodged within a broader view of ethnic identity. To show this, let us briefly examine the use of the term *race* and how it has shaped our thinking.

It is not a trivial matter to review the etymology of the word *race* as it has been applied to human beings. The term derives from the Old Italian *razza*, itself related to Semitic words for "head" or "beginning," and thus referring to a common point of descent or origin. What is particularly chilling, however, is that from this earliest use onward, race could suggest both the traits of domesticated animals (their lineage and breed) and of human beings (their origin and generations). This is no accident, for the word is indelibly stamped with ideas of purity (derivation from a common source), economics (livestock for sale or labor), and control (mastery of an identifiable species).

The application of this category to human groups has its historical origins in early modern slavery. In antiquity, the idea that some people could own others made no fundamental reference to what we think of as race. Conquered peoples or the economically vulnerable might be sold into slavery but were often not racially different from their masters and in some cases enjoyed a certain social respect. With the advent of European exploration in the late fifteenth century and the subsequent colonization especially of the Americas, however, large numbers of workers were needed to reap the economic benefits of the newly claimed lands. Race was first employed in this context to define which humans would now be viewed as labor stock to be owned and controlled for colonial settlement. It was the artificially imposed but excruciatingly painful means for enabling colonial domination and profitability.

Some may find it peculiar or even offensive to speak of race as "artificial" in its historical origins. In fact, a good bit of scholarship during the nineteenth century tried to uncover a natural reality to race through careful taxonomies of pigmentation, physical measurements, facial features, and so forth. These early anthropological studies, however, continued to be intertwined with a colonial agenda of justifying the ongoing subjugation of some peoples as inferior while valorizing others as superior. Research even within our own century has tried to legitimate these racial distinctions by appeals to human genetics. Despite all this effort, the assignment of humankind into races on allegedly biological grounds lacks all scientific support. Of course, people around the globe bear diverse appearances, but that this is due to some empirically identifiable, shared essence known as race has proven to be meaningless. Physical anthropologists have recently gone so far as to reject the validity of any such basis for race.

This is not to say that race is somehow unreal. Indeed, the very efforts to give race a *natural* basis underscore what kind of reality it truly has: a *social* category of domination and brutality. The record here is undeniable and shameful. Untold millions during the past five centuries have suffered harassment, relocation, violence, and genocide through the application of racial thinking. Such thinking was embedded in the earliest foundations of American history when whites claimed their own distinctive racial identity out of a prior willingness to enslave blacks. It continues today whenever race legitimates the view that some people are less human than others. The values we attribute to the physical features stereotyped as race persist as a reality-shaping symbol in our society, one that dare not be denied or brushed aside. It is a symbol that conveys an entire history of cruelty that various groups will forever bear as part of their self-understanding.

When we think about race in relation to the cross-cultural challenge to preaching, however, we must examine its adequacy at conveying the scope and subtleties of that challenge. First, race is so broad as a category that it masks the distinctions and divisions present within any particular racial grouping. To speak of "Asians," for example, tells us little about the profound differences between people from areas as diverse as Korea, Japan, and Laos. It also fails to reflect how "Asian" as a racial group has changed over time. The imprecision of race thus grants us little of the deep insight we need for truly cross-cultural understanding in preaching.

Second, race functions in the Unites States as a category for legal recognition in order to obtain government benefits and protections. Even so, many are realizing that race is not a fitting category for themselves. For example, *Latino* is actually an ethnic rather than a racial term, and some persons resist being tied to any one racial label at all in the census process. The legal significance of race, however, requires that those who prefer to think of themselves in ethnic or other forms of self-identification appeal to racial language in order to receive due recognition. All of this suggests that since race is so embedded in a legal framework of entitlement, it is less helpful when used in a theological framework of proclamation.

Finally, race sets up an adversarial way of viewing one another. For the historical and legal reasons mentioned above, we have been trained to understand race in terms of boundaries. Race provides the apparent basis for limiting a group to certain insiders and excluding various outsiders who stand beyond that group's visible characteristics. Not only does hostility toward other races inevitably follow from such reasoning, but also a kind of litmus test of essentials that qualify one to be truly black, white, or whatever. Hostility and essentialism, however, cannot show us how to engage diverse racial groups as people of faith. As one of our interviewees remarked, "Once you see that I'm black and a woman, what do you really know about *me?*" We seek instead a way to honor the distinctiveness of human groups without erasing the basis for making a common appeal. Beyond a doubt, race must be treated as a serious and substantive topic from the pulpit. Racial reasoning *left to itself,* however, does not illumine healthier ways toward cross-cultural preaching that are the aim of this book.

How, then, might ethnicity be more adequate than race as a way of framing an understanding of cross-cultural preaching? It does so by suggesting how the groups to which people most deeply belong shape the ways they think and act, and thus (for our purposes) how they listen and relate to preaching. As a cultural frame, ethnicity reveals these insights because it includes three components. First, ethnicity indicates a *community commitment.* Although people are typically born into ethnic groups, such groups require of their members intentional decisions and labor to continue belonging. Ethnic groups are therefore broader than just our given biological descent and origins and yet narrow enough only to involve truly significant affiliations and relationships. This is why ethnicity typically concerns smaller-scale groups than a general category like race. More important, however, is that while race is an externally imposed judgment, ethnic commitment in the long run is elective. Ethnicity is not indelible but can be supplanted due to neglect, alienation, or other stronger affiliations.

Second, ethnicity represents a *shared history,* one that includes the change and development of a people. Unlike interest groups or other casual voluntary associations, an ethnic group holds in its common memory a set of substantial experiences that are larger than any single member. The work of remaining in that group requires claiming that history and being accountable to it as the lens through which one's own life is understood. Many Serbs, for example, not only learn about the Battle of Kosovo, which took place six centuries ago, but also embrace that defeat as a paradoxical defining moment for their ethnic identity still today. Ethnicity is not involuntarily absorbed from community surroundings. Instead, it typically means being submissive to a larger identity, activating that identity in daily life, and then shouldering the burden of passing it on.

This shared history is not just a matter of words or memories, however. It quite often involves the powerful claims of a common place, a homeland that becomes a touchstone for group identity. Interviewees in strong ethnic communities noted how often they were asked at first, "Where are you *from?*" on the assumption that the answer would reveal their true commitments. (As we shall see in chapter 4, the loss of such a sense of place can also strike a devastating blow to personal identity.)

Since this shared history would have to include the harm and tragedy experienced by a group, race can be a crucial component of ethnic self-understanding. Through an ethnic frame, however, the general experience of race becomes concrete within a particular ethnic history, thereby exposing in a more potent way the role of race for a specific people. We fail to sense all that it means to be Cherokee, for example, if we only think of that group as Native American, a racial category that includes thousands of distinct groups. As an ethnic reference, however, Cherokee indicates a specific people whose history includes a home (originally the southern Appalachian region), alliances (pro-British during the American Revolution), leaders (Sequoya), factions (the Western and Eastern Bands), and, to be sure, the destructive power of racism (the Trail of Tears in the 1830s and all that has happened since). In this respect, ethnicity keeps a sharp focus on how race has been a part of Cherokee life while not reducing the group to generic labels or diminishing other important parts of their identity.

Third, ethnicity points to the *distinctive ways* of a group, the ideas and practices that embody its uniqueness. Rather than having some shared essence, members participate to a greater or lesser degree in a fluid collection of behaviors, customs, and values characteristic to that group. Ethnic identity does not at heart require a group to define itself over against another, as with the adversarial relations so central to race. Instead, an ethnic group provides through its common life a place for its members to stand, an orienting worldview that need not be contrasted with other ethnic groups. This is what makes ethnicity so important as a frame for our purposes, since this "place to stand" obviously affects the impact of preaching. (Although the distinctive ways of any ethnic group would naturally include its religious beliefs as well, these matters are special enough to merit separate treatment in chapter 5.)

As a cultural frame, ethnicity helps us to recognize the particular relations, experiences, and worldviews of those who hear our sermons. At the same time, since ethnicity is noticeable everywhere, we gain through this frame a perspective that is widely useful in many cross-cultural situations. We turn now to our interviews to see in yet greater detail how ethnic belonging can influence the task of preaching.

Group Characteristics

Ethnicity lays before us a particular journey toward understanding the group characteristics of our hearers. Those we interviewed named four markers that guided them in their own journeys. Regardless of the setting, they noted that effective ethnic preaching paid attention to trusting relationships, subgroup tensions, core values, and preaching expectations. We, too, must now stop at each of these markers for guidance, knowing they will eventually lead us into more specific preaching strategies in the final section of this chapter.

Trusting Relationships

All efforts to preach amid those from an unfamiliar ethnic background are based on relationships of trust. While some people may have natural gifts for developing these relationships, such basic matters need not be left to chance. Those we interviewed named several specific ways the preacher can take the initiative to develop a better understanding and thus signal the desire for improved relations.

The most direct approach is simply the *intentional study* of an ethnic group to understand its background and place. This was often stated in linguistic terms like "being fluent in" or "increasingly conversant with" another culture. At one level, this requires the disciplined research to uncover a group's history and geography, not just what it says of itself, but also how it has related to other ethnic groups. Awareness of current affairs is also important, however, and can be gained through ethnic magazines, newspapers, radio stations, or television programs. The archives of ethnic resources can also be found in unexpected places.

One preacher with many Lakota members was surprised to discover that many ethnic stories crucial to the worldview of her listeners were now stored on various Native American web sites.

Two other forms of intentional study are more demanding but were also highly recommended. One is actually to travel to the ethnic homeland of your hearers, preferably in their company. Though costly in time and money, such journeys were richly repaid with a deepened grasp of specific places and events that shaped those people. The chance for shared experiences and strong emotional bonds with members also gave a basis upon which future preaching could build. The other form of intentional study involved, where applicable, learning the language of an ethnic group. Our interviewees were quick to point out how very difficult this is. Actual bilingual communication takes a long time to develop and is never truly finished. Moreover, a single ethnic group in the United States often includes generations with quite different competencies in a home language, from the elderly who may know little English to young children who may know little else. Even so, interest in another language can also be shown by using it in greetings and sayings, or by examining a few words from it in a sermon. Knowing the language, like knowing the land, can at least indicate a basic concern for the marks that bind and preserve an ethnic heritage.

Intentional study in all these ways not only awakens the preacher to ethnic issues and concerns, but also opens the door for deeper relationships with members of the group itself. One person noted that once he became familiar enough with Japanese events and culture to mention these in private conversations with members, his interest was matched by their rich sharing of personal experiences. Being a student of an ethnic group opens the door to being a student of the specific people among whom you serve. This leads, then, to a second way of building trust, that of *participatory contact* with an ethnic group. The impact of this way upon establishing trust is nicely summarized in the words of a pastor serving in a Puerto Rican setting:

> There are two things that people say about me when they introduce me as their pastor. One thing they say is "She speaks Spanish very well—better than we do!" which is true in a lot of cases. But the second thing they always say is, "She lives in the neighborhood." They never feel the need to explain that I am a woman, and the fact that I am Anglo is something that surprises people if they notice. But living in the neighborhood is a sign of commitment. For anybody who works cross-culturally, it is not even an option. It is unquestionably a given.

Indeed, everyone we interviewed in an ethnically distinct setting said there was no substitute for a daily, honest, and deep engagement in the life the community.

Beyond the rather obvious matter of living where members do, other suggestions for participatory contact were offered. Regular sites of ordinary public contact are important places to frequent. In general, though, one interviewee urged: "Take part in the activities that they are taking part in, and be interested and asking questions and trying to understand. And I don't mean trying to be the people, as if you can ever become one of them, but being with them, understanding that you come from a different perspective and have some different ideas and values and experiences." This advice is intriguing. An inquisitive and risking spirit is surely needed. At the same time, however, enough self-awareness is needed to claim one's own personal identity without apology. We are bid to show a curious blend of humility and strength.

Where are some of these regular sites of ordinary public contact in ethnic communities? Schools are certainly important in this regard as places of youth development as well as sports and entertainment events. Schools also become a window for viewing the serious social needs of an ethnic group, since challenges facing the youth are often of great concern to the entire community. Whatever places serve as an ethnic market (stores, streets, weekly fairs, or outdoor sales) are also important venues to meet people in their daily routines. The preacher is encountered in such places outside of any "official" role. A lowered intimidation factor means you may be perceived as more approachable and open to casual conversation (which, in many ethnic communities, is an art form in itself). Some preachers with whom we spoke encouraged visiting people at their places of work, assuming such visits are possible. One last place of ordinary contact, and perhaps most important of all, is in the home itself. The chance to meet an entire family, view special treasures (artwork or albums, for example), and be welcomed in someone else's space is an important bond not to be missed. Interviewees often remarked about how people from certain ethnic backgrounds take special pride in having the preacher in the home, viewing it as a sign of honor and an opportunity to be lavish. Moreover, home visitation gives further insight into crucial cultural aspects of meal practice, hospitality, conversation, respect, and daily routines.

Other forms of contact involve participation in special occasions such as festivals, anniversaries, or funerals. Some of these may require a specific invitation, but our contacts revealed that exclusive events were less common than one might first imagine. The pastor, even if not expected to be at such events (let alone filling some official role), is almost always welcome. These times are very important for the preacher because they reveal an ethnic group at its key transitions, either remembering something from the past (such as a commemoration) or enacting some passage in the present (such as a death). How such transitions are handled, emotions expressed, and experiences drawn into a group's shared memory can be rich points of contact for later proclamation.

Since such special events can be notoriously difficult to understand, some ministers urged turning to "culture brokers," members of the ethnic group who will interpret what is happening. Turning to someone else for basic questions or to test emerging perceptions is another act of humility essential to multi-ethnic understanding. It also honors an ethnic group as being truly competent to speak for itself, with the further benefit of building support for the preacher who is trying hard to "get it right." At the same time, however, some have cautioned about undue reliance upon such brokers and have noted the need to check what you learn with several sources. One reason for this is the simple fact that, as said in chapter 1, culture is not monolithic. There are likely many perspectives on what a particular ethnic heritage means. Another reason for caution is that some culture brokers may have vested interests they wish to advance through a close alliance with the preacher. Provided one consults people broadly representative of the ethnic group in question, however, these concerns probably do not present a serious barrier.

Besides intentional study and participatory contact, one last way to garner trusting relationships is through *symbolic markers*. Indeed, much of what we have discussed so far is already symbolic, and in no cheap or superficial way. Learning about a group and knowing its rhythms already symbolizes a kind of concern that cannot be dismissed. *Trying* to learn a language or *displaying* in your office the ethnic periodicals you read will surely be noticed, according to those with whom we spoke. Beyond these, though, they also suggested several other kinds of symbols that might not usually be considered.

Many placed ethnic artwork prominently in the worship space. Banners that read "Welcome" in many different languages were quite popular and effective, as were paintings or posters displaying people of diverse ethnic appearances. Some sanctuaries were outfitted with a large number of national flags as signs of the many ethnic groups who worshiped there. Other congregations with only a few dominant ethnic groups used artwork from those groups (such as textiles, ceramics, flower arrangements, or color motifs) to set a tone within the room. Even the attire worn by the preacher or other worship leaders (like the choir) could reflect an ethnic heritage.

Such symbols require great planning and care, of course, but once in place may need little further attention. Other symbols are more active in nature, such as specially planned celebrations. Obviously, it is possible to honor significant ethnic festivals within the life of the congregation (national holidays or saints days). But another powerful way of building both the ethnic identity within a congregation and a broader understanding beyond it is through joint fellowship events with groups of a different heritage. A Lutheran pastor serving a largely Korean congregation spoke of a Reformation Sunday celebration jointly held with a nearby German congregation.

> Then we had an Oktoberfest luncheon afterwards. We made it intentionally ethnic,
> but we did it in such a way that we celebrated our unity in diversity. We took an

example that everybody could understand: cabbage. Sauerkraut and kimchi both have cabbage as a common element, and so they on the surface appear to be different, but in actuality are one and the same. So doing something like that where we drew on both traditions, we celebrated our unity in Christ.

It might seem like a long way from cabbage to preaching that is able to reach across ethnic differences. Sometimes, however, the trip is made easier by little, everyday symbols of basic recognition that can eventually lead to a deeper understanding, even from the pulpit.

Attention to trusting relationships is its own reward, of course, but it also contributes directly and indirectly to preaching itself. Knowing more about an ethnic group obviously gives substantive materials that permit an immediate connection with the lives of our hearers both before and during the sermon. Mentioning these insights is also an important way of validating ethnic groups that have often been ignored or undervalued. One pastor, for example, said that he regularly referred to specific tribal or clan customs in sermons because simply mentioning these traditions often was enough to give hope to his hearers and restore a lost sense of dignity. Perhaps the most striking thing about relationships of trust, however, is the change they impart to the preacher. Biblical texts begin to speak in vibrant new ways when the preacher is committed to a particular ethnic group. Moreover, preachers often told of their surprising realization that their own preaching had dramatically changed in style and content once they had become invested in the fate of a people different from themselves. In other words, this is the third kind of "recognition" we spoke of in chapter 1, the rethinking it brings upon ourselves.

A final remark is in order. Those we interviewed noted the paradoxical relation of trust and knowledge, both of which are essential for cross-ethnic understanding to flourish. On the one hand, a group will not trust you unless you take the time to know them first. Taking time to learn about others is, as we have remarked, a strong symbol that in itself engenders trust. On the other hand, it is nearly impossible to know a group well unless they trust you first. All you can hope to learn will come from external sources until group members are themselves willing to disclose more fully who they are. This paradoxical and reciprocal tension between knowledge and trust points to the need for two dispositions, we were told. The first is to have *initiative,* taking the first step to know and the first risk toward trust. The second is to have *integrity,* showing that you are a trustworthy person whose insights about others will not be used to inflict harm. Initiative and integrity are therefore the ways we prove *ourselves* to be neighbor to others.

Subgroup Tensions

The more aware you become of the ethnic identities within a group, the more likely you are to notice the vast differences and strong divisions there as well. Several people we interviewed who served in Latino settings, for example, reported that their congregations appeared homogeneous to outsiders. They in fact contained in one case six separate ethnic identities, in another seventeen, and in still another as many as twenty-two! One self-identified "Asian" congregation included among its Chinese members alone four distinct dialect groups. Even rather small urban churches could boast a dizzying mix of refugees from Eastern Europe, sub-Saharan Africa, and Native reservations in the upper Midwest. This only goes to underscore what we said earlier, that culture (here in its ethnic frame) is plural.

Ethnic subgroups within a single assembly have their roots in many different sources. One of the most apparent is a linguistic dialect or accent, itself a reflection of a distinct geography or history. Though these can quickly indicate to members who differs from whom, such cues often elude the pastor who does not share the ethnic heritage involved. Closely related to verbal matters are regional differences, the specific country or area within it that someone counts as a homeland. Some pastors we met have been shocked in recent years to see long-buried regional hostilities flare up in their congregations due to interethnic conflicts half a world away. Different generations also produce ethnic subgroups. Those more closely tied to an ethnic homeland due to age or recent immigration construct ethnic identity using different resources than those vigorously adapting to a new situation (see chapter 4). Separate generations can also reflect class distinctions of wealth, education, and status (see chapter 3). Ethnic subgroups can also follow religious lines. People from an otherwise similar ethnic heritage may know very different experiences of the church or of other religious traditions that result in quite particular views of how to be the church now (see chapter 5). Finally, subgroups can develop due to the high value many ethnic groups place upon the family. The clan of your biological or legal relatives can demand a loyalty that leads to factions among otherwise ethnically similar persons.

Given all these factors, it is perhaps more surprising that ethnically diverse congregations can stay together at all. Sometimes they do not. One pastor with a lifetime of service in both Chinese and Korean groups contrasted the two by saying that the latter, in his experience, was more likely to let differences lead to schism. Another person recalled similar tendencies in a particular Latino setting whenever class or nationality began to predominate. Such cases notwithstanding, there are many compelling forces that hold ethnic subgroups together in congregations. The irony is that they are often the very same forces as those that threaten to tear them apart.

Even though linguistic cues, for example, expose different subgroups, a common language can also bind disparate groups in important ways. When people feel adrift in virtually every other part of their lives, the chance to worship in one's home language can be a profound gift, even if that language is spoken in unusual ways. There are also common histories that unite ethnically diverse subgroups, albeit haunting ones. What holds some subgroups together may not be a shared time and place but a similar experience of oppression or displacement. The specifics differ from group to group, but the common story tells the same suffering and sorrow. Ethnic subgroups, therefore, may lack a common place to stand but can still share a common will to survive. Another unifying feature in diverse congregations is their role as enclaves of support and nurture. Subgroups in a particular neighborhood may be unquestionably distinct, but they must all deal with that same neighborhood, with the congregation itself as a means for that sort of engagement. Since subgroups also form along clan lines, and since congregations are places such relations are nurtured, ethnic subgroups stay together in churches that grant broad support to families. Finally, despite all their distinctions, ethnic subgroups still claim to assemble as church. Even in light of the potential for human sin and division, these groups gather as people of faith who await from God a hope beyond the wounds and hatred they have already known. Perhaps most basic of all, this unity of God is the gift that preserves congregations amid their ethnic differences.

We have raised this issue of subgroup tensions because it was such a widespread concern among those we interviewed. At the same time, no one claimed that there was something to be done about this situation. Subgroups and the tensions between them were not seen as something to be "fixed." Of course, some congregations have tensions so great that trained intervention may be needed—a matter clearly beyond the scope of this book. In most cases, however, the preacher simply faces a congregation of delightfully bewildering complexity. It is simply important, our informants said, to be aware at the beginning that subgroup tensions exist. Romanticized and idealistic hopes for interethnic harmony are not only unhelpful but paternalistic. Needed instead is a basic realism about the tensions that exist, as well as the creative energy to use them instructively and fruitfully. Ethnic subgroups, taken seriously, can be a sign that enriches the church and honors the distinctive places where all of us, even preachers, must stand.

Core Values

Earlier, we argued for the usefulness of ethnicity as a cultural frame because it conveys the shared history of a group (change and development) and its distinctive ways (ideas and practices). This sense of past and place has a profound symbolic power, giving people a way of orienting their individual lives in relation to the core values of a larger ethnic identity. Obviously, we cannot hope to catalog every sort of core value that might be important to consider in ethnically aware preaching, for it would be extremely difficult to do justice to that task even within a single situation. We were able to discern throughout our interviews, however, several broad contours to a terrain you could explore further in your own specific setting. In effect, our interviewees said that ethnic characteristics could be better understood by focusing on four areas of core values that were manifested in many specific ways in any one group.

The first area to notice is the value given to *personal identity*. To illustrate, one Hispanic woman described a typical adjustment she makes when preaching in an Anglo setting.

> When I'm referring to identity in a sermon for a Hispanic group, somehow I have to bring in the family theme or some family focus there, because that's what our identity's based on. I will not do that—I'm sorry—with an Anglo group. I would talk there more in individual terms when I talk about identity before Christ or whatever way I'm using identity. In the one case I would have to be mindful that identity has something to do with family, but in the other I would have to know that it has more to do with individuals. Being from a Hispanic perspective, I've had to learn that when I preach to them.

Whether or not her characterization of personal identity in these groups is accurate, what matters is the sense that identity stands in a continuum from individual to corporate. The values of any ethnic group can therefore be better grasped by noticing the place of personal identity along that continuum.

In a more corporate understanding, it is only natural that the most significant social relations provide the strongest basis for identity. The remark above and many others like it emphasized the role of family relationships in defining personal identity. A preacher in a largely Chinese congregation noted the importance of the elderly, while another in a Latino setting stressed the place of mothers and fathers, and still another pastor pointed to the worth of children for several Native American groups in the upper Midwest. Such family figures were not only central to human nurture but also defined the horizons of past and future and therefore affected the identity of every person in the community.

In somewhat broader scope, the social relations found in congregation and neighborhood are also significant for personal identity. Greetings and other interpersonal affirmations that characterize some ethnic community settings (not to mention styles of worship) show a dense web of corporate identity formation and nurture. When such webs then become strained or broken, the pain is not only felt between people but also at the very heart of the personal self. One pastor, referring to a parishioner who had known such pain, mentioned how that theme became important in preaching.

> This person was telling me that it's been a long time since she had spoken to a relative of hers. So this sense of relationship is a two-edged sword. It's there, but it's also very divisive. When that relationship is broken, then the whole life goes out the window. What I did [in the sermon] is I talked about how this relationship—broken relationship—had made this one person I talked to feel not good about *herself*. The

crazy things that we do that prevent us from leading a meaningful life *and* having a healthy relationship with *one another!*

Comments like this underscore that all persons bear a socially established identity whether that fact is lifted up within their ethnic group or not. For this same reason, ethnic groups often reveal a great deal about their treasured values in the way they portray personal identity.

A second area to notice is the value given to *language use*. The maintenance of strong corporate bonds in an ethnic group does not happen by accident. Among other things, it relies heavily upon language that easily and vividly brings people together—oral language. Some ethnic groups may lean more heavily on written and abstracted communication, but our informants made it clear that this was the exception rather than the rule. The centrality of speech and listening was obvious in quite diverse ethnic settings.

Orality has already received such vast scholarly attention that we cannot hope to reproduce those insights here. Perhaps the most noted scholar in this area, Walter Ong (see Suggested Readings), showed that language that relies on sound alone is charged with energy and, at the same time, extremely fragile. That is, speech has an immediacy and dynamism that comes from lasting only for the period of its utterance. For the same reason, however, oral forms of language also place special demands upon the memory, since anything not remembered will be lost. As a result, groups that are predominantly oral have a greater concern for concrete and memorable language, a give-and-take form of reasoning, and a conservatizing approach to whatever has been heard and remembered. These same characteristics appeared time and again in our interviews.

As we have already noted, many ethnic groups rely upon languages other than English. The chances for misunderstanding are replete wherever two language worlds are at stake, but often the problem has more to do with orality than vocabulary. Regardless of the specific language, orally oriented groups pay much closer attention to the lifeworld of their members. Specific contexts and practices come to matter far more than abstract terminology, and so misunderstandings can result when a term from one concrete setting is used in a way alien to that setting. A preacher in a Vietnamese church that operated *entirely in English* recalled his struggle with using the word *bread* in a sermon. The problem was not that the word failed to make sense, but that bread is used by Vietnamese as a frivolous pastry rather than a source of basic sustenance. Due to its oral orientation, this ethnic group heard "bread" concretely and so gave it a quite unintended meaning.

One reason orally oriented groups pay such attention to the lifeworld of members is that oral communication relies upon close physical proximity. You can only communicate orally with those who are together in one place to hear what is being said. This is why orality carries such a dynamic charge, for living groups of adjacent people actively participate in how a message unfolds by means of vocal responses, body postures, facial expressions, and so forth. African American call-response preaching, for example, has long been noted as a premier example of this orally attuned use of give-and-take speech amid a distinctive, vibrant gathering. Apart from special events, however, other orally oriented groups display this socially participatory language in ordinary forms like everyday conversation. In a part-Latino, part-Anglo congregation, the pastor recalled a lively dialogue *after* the worship about a word used during the sermon.

> They said "What are you trying to say?" So here we were, trying to deal theologically and culturally with this word *righteousness*. It needed about three or four sentences to talk about how, first of all, righteousness is a gift from God, and I think we talked about living the way God would want us to do, and also the word *blessing* was involved with that. So as a community, we came up with a pretty good working definition. But it took a conversation rather than a single word, about a half hour to get this concept there.

The view that meaning emerges through interaction rather than by reading or from authorities may be unfamiliar to some ethnic groups. At the same time, though, it reinforces how language use reveals something about group values.

Especially for ethnic groups that have faced suffering in both the past and the present, oral language has been a particularly valuable resource. With no written histories to preserve key memories, such groups depend upon passing down stories and traditions to be learned by all members. These procedures are often the most readily available tool for keeping ethnic identity alive. One pastor who served in an Ojibwa community remarked: "The most important thing that I found that I need to do with these people is learn to tell stories well. These people are story tellers, and they often tell their own personal stories over and over and over again. And in some mysterious way, that seems to connect with these people. It doesn't have to be a new story. It can be the same story, because that's what they do." Note here especially the importance of repetition. While societies oriented toward writing tend to privilege novelty and innovation, orally rooted groups treasure the repeated and trustworthy. On the one hand, this can seem to outsiders like being mired in tradition. On the other hand, however, this conservatizing approach is a powerful strategy for survival. Indeed, the only form of resistance available to many groups during centuries of harm has been the oral narratives told to preserve and restore ethnic solidarity.

A third area to notice is the value given to *time use,* a matter closely related to language use. Simply put, speech takes time. In orally oriented groups where corporate identity and meaning emerge interactively through retold narratives, we ought to expect a distinctive tempo to life. How can anyone say in advance when a conversation will be over? It is finished when it has built the relationships and acknowledged the needs that it set out to do, and not before. Our interviewees therefore often remarked about a fluid sense of time in worship and other events among orally attuned ethnic groups. Groups *not* so attuned tended to measure time by external standards: clocks, schedules, agendas. Oral societies, however, were more willing to dally and take the time to do what was necessary for the good of the group. This affected not only the ending time of events but their starting time as well. A meeting, or for that matter a sermon, would begin only once everyone had finally arrived and the participants seemed to be ready. This sense of the group and its moods was but another way that attention to the life-world of the members so typical with oral societies came to the fore.

Besides beginnings and endings, the overall duration of an event also revealed certain ethnic values. This is once again related to language use. In orally sensitive groups, repetition is a valued part of speech because it aids the memory, giving the ears (the only means for reception) more than one chance to hear what is being conveyed. There is a greater expectation on speakers, therefore, to take their time in making points, state them several times over, and delight in the digressions and playfulness of language that make speech memorable. These strategies take time, of course, and may seem inefficient to ethnic groups oriented more toward an economy of spoken words and the use of efficient, written texts.

Some of our respondents also noted the relation between time use in certain ethnic groups and the ways they participate in an event. Ethnic patterns were sometimes apparent about the permissibility to enter or leave (and often repeatedly) during an event. One ethnic group might enforce a strict and steady level of attention by all participants (sometimes accompanied by silence and attentive postures), while another might allow for inattention and distraction (including the freedom to get up and move around as necessary). Such matters expose not just different attitudes about time in ethnic communities, but especially what a gathering itself represents for those groups.

A final area to notice is the value given to *particularity,* a consequence of the other values listed above. Wherever face-to-face relationships and community maintenance receive greater attention, the concrete aspects of life will also be in the foreground. One Puerto Rican pastor commented on his own ethnicity in a way that seemed to fit many of the groups we encountered: "When you talk about issues and things that are very, very important to us, we tend to interpret them first in the personal sense, and the abstract takes second level. So you have to speak diplomatically but very concretely."

Unsurprisingly, the value of particularity can be vividly seen in how an ethnic group recounts its own history. Although every ethnic history is particular, dominant groups have had little reason to preserve specific accounts other than their own in the official histories they have authored. On the other hand, marginalized groups with a more precarious past have taken great pains to remember the details of their particular journey. Preachers serving in a wide range of marginalized ethnic groups told us how their members filtered nearly all they heard through that group's entire, often centuries-long experience of hostility and subjugation. This only reinforces our earlier comment that knowing ethnic history is essential.

That history has not ended, of course, and so another place particularity is valued is in reference to the contemporary treatment of an ethnic group. Ethnic identity in American society is not an abstract idea or an analytical concept but relates to specific kinds of treatment. Immigration policy, for example, is not a matter of laws passed in distant halls of power but of Immigration and Naturalization Service officers in your neighborhood or workplace and what they actually do to those you know personally. Particularity is the window through which many ethnic groups have come to view the American experience. In a similar and still more troubling way, particularity is the window through which these same groups have come to view the church, which has often been an accomplice in ethnic alienation and abuse. Finally, particularity describes the daily life within the community, including the presence or absence of violence, substance abuse, decent housing, and so forth. Particularity is therefore a point of contact both between an ethnic group and larger realities (such as nation and church) and among its own members (common neighborhood realities). Such particular forms of treatment bind a group together and are the focus of its oral discourse. This simply reinforces our earlier comment that full participation in the life of the community is essential.

Once the value of particularity is appreciated, certain implications for preaching immediately follow. A white preacher in a largely African American congregation began to connect specific phases of that group's background (such as the "middle passage" of the slave trade and modern efforts at affirmative action) with biblical texts and spiritual issues, to powerful effect. Other preachers spoke of mentioning specific ethnic figures (leaders or saints) or occasions (commemorations or festivals) that provided striking analogies with contemporary situations. None of these, however, were gimmicks designed to pander to an ethnic group. Instead, they simply located the sermon within a community discourse that was already underway and itself quite particular. Attention to the particularities of a group also held another intriguing potential. In some cases, specific matters in one group (such as histories of forced migration or current experiences of mistreatment) forged unexpected links with the particularities of other groups. The result was both new partnerships and a broader sense of church.

Preaching Expectations

Before turning directly to preaching strategies, a final group characteristic in the frame of ethnicity involves expectations about the task of preaching itself. There are many connections between these expectations and our previous remarks about relationships, subgroups, and values. For example, the need to build trust and knowledge in an ethnic group has implications for what these groups expect of their preachers. In a similar way, language use in an ethnic group is further reflected in which scriptural texts it favors and which sermon designs it prefers. In broad scope, then, three areas of preaching expectations were most frequently mentioned by our respondents: the view of the preacher, the use of scripture, and the sermon itself.

By contrast with their experiences in so-called traditional white congregations (a broad characterization, to be sure), our interviewees uniformly remarked that close-knit, nondominant ethnic groups view the *preacher* with higher regard. In many different Native American groups great honor is accorded the spiritually gifted since they will help guide others in spiritual quests. A wide range of East Asian groups impute both high status and vast responsibility to their religious leaders. Even among Latino groups like Puerto Ricans where authority figures are regularly critiqued, the preacher is still granted a large measure of unchallenged respect. Set against an American religious ethos often skeptical about those in power and fiercely democratic about clergy-lay relations, such a view of the preacher may seem odd and even awesome. Interviews were therefore also sprinkled with reminders of the pitfalls of this view, especially the risk that elevated pastoral authority can be abused. What preachers in cross-cultural situations need to realize, then, is that the preaching task is granted an official power fraught with vast potentials and ominous dangers.

One reason certain ethnic groups value preachers so highly has to do with ethnically defined ways authority is ascribed to some persons and not others. Chronological age is often part of the formula, since being older supposedly brings the experience and wisdom that merit respect. Younger preachers may still be granted authority if they bear the confidence and maturity one would find with an older person. (It is not incidental, in this regard, that we commonly heard how many ethnic groups expect their pastors to adopt a conservative attire typical of the style of elders!) Being from within the ethnic group itself is also part of the pattern for ascribing authority, since groups tend to believe and therefore entrust with power those who are more like themselves. (Some ethnic groups are just the reverse, however, willingly granting power to outsiders in order to avoid the clan factionalism that accompanies leadership from within.) Related to this, of course, are matters of gender and its place in an ethnic community. It comes as no surprise that ethnic groups steeped in patriarchy more readily ascribe public status and overt power to men.

Since authority comes through these ethnically defined ways of ascribing power, does this simply mean that only the older men from within a group can be powerful as preachers? If so, then effective proclamation amid those whose ethnicity differs from our own would be beyond reach. However, our interviewees recalled these ascribed aspects of authority not just because they had faced them but especially because they found creative strategies beyond them. One younger, white, female preacher serving a joint Thai Don and Laotian congregation recounted how her members wanted to honor her authority in a way not otherwise known within their ethnic heritages.

> This community is pretty much a patriarchal community. But beyond that was a sense that whoever the religious leader was, it was just a given that this person would be respected and that person's words would be truth. Well, our first Christmas party, which was part of the religious celebration for all of us, was put on by the Lao group. The group set up the tables, a whole row of tables on one side of the room and a whole row of tables on the other side of the room. And they expected that the men would sit in one row and the women would sit in the other. And when I came in, they thought, "What are we going to do?" because if I was truly recognized as the religious leader, I would have to sit with the men. And they realized, well, I'm not a man, so in their culture I should sit with the women. So they brought the tables together into a U-shape and had me sit right in the middle intersection, so all the men were on one side of me and all the women were on the other!

This creative effort cannot be explained in terms of ascription, the ethnic "givens" of who will have authority and who will not. In fact, this pastor posed a dilemma because her persistence at knowing and building up the members now needed to be honored in a seating arrangement that could display her authority while preserving the group's values. In other words, the heightened status of this preacher (and others like her) depends not only on what an ethnic group is willing to ascribe but also on what caring pastoral work is able to achieve.

One way to achieve greater pastoral status is, as we have said earlier, through establishing trust. As an ethnic group hears a preacher speaking in ways it can grasp (concretely, accessibly, and in some cases even in its home language), it is more willing to grant appropriate authority. Passionate preaching that integrates preacher and message also enhances pastoral esteem, as does a mutual style of leadership that seeks the gifts of all the members. A preacher in a Filipino community echoed many others in noting that regular participation in community life not only respects an ethnic group but is reciprocated by them as well. Our interviewees also added that longer service within an ethnic group produces greater authority, since the length of tenure symbolizes commitment. In all these ways and others mentioned earlier in this chapter, deepened trust by a group results in heightened authority for the preacher.

Besides trust, however, the preacher's authority within an ethnic group is achieved through serious attention to personal character. Some of this demands nothing more or less than being a public model within the community. Appropriate language or ethical behavior in daily life are a few of the ways this is signified.

Beyond these basic standards, however, pastoral authority is distinctively affected by the link between personal character and the preaching task itself. That is, many ethnic groups view the preacher as a channel of the sacred itself (as with several Native American groups) or the bearer of holy words (as with some Korean and several Latino groups). As a result, the preacher is not just speaking about God but, insofar as scripture is given new utterance, symbolizing the divine voice. For this reason the personal character of the preacher becomes for such groups a living text, an embodiment of the preaching, or a sermon in its own right. At stake here is something other than simplistic calls for preachers to be morally consistent or even sinless. Instead, the sermon alone is incomplete apart from the preacher's life, as one pastor in a Japanese setting remarked. Personal character can become a testimony that rounds out the oral proclamation, and the extent to which it actually achieves this leads to a greater degree of pastoral authority.

The sense that personal character embodies the text leads us naturally into a second area of preaching expectations in many ethnic groups: the use of *scripture*. As with the view of the preacher so also the view of scripture is elevated. The relation between the two is quite close, since pastoral authority in these groups is typically rooted in a scriptural authority that treats the Bible as divine speech and thus unlike any other book. As a consequence, pastors spoke of the need to ground their preached remarks in scriptural references so that both the message and the one speaking it would receive credibility. In addition, they pointed out that such a heightened sense of scriptural authority leads to a special sort of hermeneutic. Texts are interpreted in many ethnic groups largely as they stand, with a plain, commonsense understanding. The tendency in academic biblical interpretation to adopt an analytical, critical stance about texts generally had little place in the congregations we came to know. This is not intended as counsel for simplistic literal interpretation but instead acknowledges that scripture use is expected to connect with the lives of hearers. One respondent serving in a multi-ethnic congregation with a long history especially in the Japanese community remarked:

> I think the Japanese seem to talk more about contemplative things, spiritual things in nature just because of their language. Every Bible study for us becomes a time of confession and being touched by the Spirit and elated and warmed with such a wonderful affirmation of God's presence in our hearts, in our lives. I try to avoid going into a sort of analytical aspect. The aim is to dig deeper into the spiritual and unconscious, into our hearts, instead of ending with the comparative cultural and historical analysis. I used to do it that way, but I find it more possible for people to read the Bible as a *lectio divina*.

Note that the assumption here is that the plainer reading of a text is potentially the richer one. As puzzling as that perspective may seem to readers trained in historical critical methods, it was nonetheless prevalent in the many groups encompassed in our interview sample. Another pastor experienced with preaching in Native American, Laotian, Latino, and Hawaiian settings said that he had encountered similar resistance to analytical interpretation in them all, adding, "It is very much a Euro-American way of doing things, this analyzing, separating, and then coming to a new conclusion. But then, I think there's a whole lot of white people who would have the same problem."

Another similarity between this use of scripture and our earlier remarks about the view of the preacher is the potential for abuse of authority. When biblical texts are both highly valued and yet interpreted at a basic, unelaborated level, they can easily be distorted toward harmful ends. In naming the problem, preachers noted several self-corrective devices used by the ethnic communities they served to guard against this danger. Some discouraged the use of extremely brief biblical texts as the basis for a sermon, insisting upon hearing longer or multiple passages handled in their broad literary contexts. Others had a well-established practice of using study groups to explore texts with the pastor prior to the preaching, not least of all to voice the group's perceptions of the preaching texts. Many looked for biblical texts to be presented in instructional and expository ways within sermons. Such groups did not expect preachers to give answers as much as open up new challenges and tensions within the texts themselves. "They do not want the sense in any way, shape, or form that I am speaking down to them," said one pastor in a Lakota congregation. "I can do the teaching, but it *has* to come in a way that we are discovering the text together." In this mutual enterprise, congregations found a path between an authoritarian use of scripture and interpretive methods that they felt did violence to the Bible. By being drawn into a natural questioning of the texts, groups developed the skills for a closer, nuanced reading that still honored the full authority of the Word.

This, in turn, leads to the last of the preaching expectations mentioned by our respondents: the *sermon* itself. It is only natural that ethnic groups who derive the preacher's authority from biblical authority would expect the preaching event itself to be profoundly stamped by scripture. What this specifically meant in many groups was that the sermon would have a strongly educational aim. This should not be understood as unloading information about the Bible but instead equipping hearers to engage in a lively struggle with the text. The emotional and cognitive impact of a text were so intertwined in such preaching that one member of a joint Latino and Anglo congregation told her pastor, "Now it makes sense. You explain the scriptures and it touches me, so I walk away with something new." Sermons with this sort of purpose were warmly welcomed, whereas lectures about biblical themes and figures were not.

Preaching was also expected to make regular reference to the actual lives and experiences of the hearers, and for two reasons. On the one hand, actual connections were thereby concretely made with the daily life of members, including the injustices and hardships they suffered. This simply echoes our earlier remarks about the value of particularity. On the other hand, these references served to make the sermon more accessible to listeners. In hearing about people like themselves, members were on familiar turf and usually in a language style with which they were accustomed. (In the case of several different Latino groups, for example, this meant that a longer sermon was assumed as well.) This echoes our earlier remarks about the value of language use, especially orality. A woman who served an urban setting comprised of several Native American groups recalled an early discovery about worship in her congregation: "Their bulletin referred to what we would comfortably know as the sermon as 'the story time.' I asked them about that and I said, 'I assume that this is where the preaching is,' and they said, 'Yes, it is.' Coming out of a strong oral tradition in many of our tribal traditions, this period of learning would have to come through storytelling." To relate the rich experiences of a group to its treasured book requires something beyond the dryness of a lecture or the shrillness of a diatribe.

One remaining expectation about the sermon concerns group participation. It might be commonplace to assume that most nondominant ethnic groups actively participate in sermons, but it would also be incorrect. We discovered instead a wide range of very different emotional and physical responses during the sermon. Some were overt and verbal in nature (widespread shouts of "Amen!" or "Hallelujah!"), others were restrained yet obvious (quiet crying or softly spoken remarks), still others were quite subtle in posture or facial expression (wrinkled noses, folded arms, raised eyebrows), and still others had no externally visible reaction at all. Of course, members of most every group expected to participate deeply in the sermon; the point is that there was simply no one way of doing so.

For this reason, several interviewees urged preachers unfamiliar with an ethnic group to learn typical responses by watching how participants react to other speakers in the community such as teachers, politicians, or labor leaders. They also reported that most groups, including those with highly noticeable participation, were nonetheless leery about speakers who pandered to such tendencies for the sake of immediate reaction. Certainly good preaching must be adaptive to the mood of the gathering but never in order to manipulate that mood. In addition, some pastors stressed that responses often did not occur during the sermon itself but in the hymns and prayers later in worship or through conversations later in the week. Virtually everyone who spoke on the subject added that, regardless of response type, the ethnic groups they knew were as concerned with the lasting as with the immediate impact.

Preaching Strategies

Based upon the group characteristics mentioned above, we turn now to advice about preaching strategies. Astute readers may already have guessed some of these recommendations by now, because we learned them through the same process that showed us the group characteristics of ethnicity in the first place. Indeed, our larger intent is to model an inductive approach that first asks deeply about a group through a particular cultural frame and then builds carefully upon those insights toward better ways of preaching. To do otherwise would hastily and inappropriately impose ready-made techniques upon complex cross-cultural challenges. A more patient study, by contrast, has made clear to us important strategies about speech genres, engaging moves, artistic treasures, and active texts that seem especially relevant within the frame of ethnicity.

Speech Genres

We have already noted that language is one of several important ways an ethnic group reinforces and conveys a worldview. This is obvious when groups preserve a language that differs from that of the larger society in order to maintain group identity. Even when an ethnic group's language is identical with that society, however, its special use within the group may convey deep symbols and meanings unavailable to anyone else. Knowing this, the preacher faces the challenge of how to speak without creating confusion or unintended harm.

Such misunderstandings happen in well-intentioned ways. A common example from our interviewees concerned their own gaffes with using humor. These preachers were quite aware that an appropriate humor was helpful in building connections and displaying a range of emotions from the pulpit. To their dismay, however, they also were reminded that humor in any language often relies upon subtle layers of meaning or a reversal of expectations that may not be evident to every hearer. One person recalled:

> There was an event I referred to in the news that was somewhat light-hearted. I didn't spend a lot of time describing it but assumed it was a point of contact that we all could relate to. The traditionally English-speaking part of the congregation responded immediately and laughed, but the Korean members who were there didn't. I noticed the differences in response and the puzzlement on their faces. It was just on the margin enough and the way I expressed it was subtle enough that they didn't catch the point that I was saying. They heard it literally and understood what the words meant but didn't catch the double meaning.

This can cut both ways, of course. A preacher may try to be humorous and instead elicit only blank stares, or wish to be serious but produce knowing glances and unexpected snickers.

These kinds of difficulties with language need not lead to despair about cross-cultural preaching. Instead, they caution us to seek distinctive devices for speaking that can minimize confusion while appealing broadly to a variety of hearers. Our respondents named certain speech genres (ways of arranging what they said) that they found especially helpful in this regard. In particular, they suggested devices ranging from the large-scale to the rather fine-grained.

First among these for virtually every ethnic group our respondents mentioned was the use of *narrative*. Some said this was because narratives created "a vicarious experience that helps people get inside the scripture and draws them into the story." Others pointed out that "if a story is told well, it will speak to the heart, not to the mind only, but to the whole person." Still others singled out the inherent ease in following a narrative, enabling hearers from a variety of ethnic backgrounds to stay on track easily. Finally, in some cases an ethnic group itself might expect that anything worth knowing would be told in a story, and anyone worth hearing would be a good storyteller. In summary, narrative is an effective genre in multi-ethnic preaching because it creates an accessible event of total engagement that has the ring of authenticity.

Closely related to narrative is the use of *images* as a way of speaking. Whereas narratives unfold across time like a drama, images are more like a snapshot that conveys a moment of time in all its richness. Narratives might use images, but images are not merely decorative examples. They are distinctly able to create a point of sensory, emotional, or experiential connection with hearers. One of the key mechanisms by which they do this, according to our informants, is by being specific. The paradox is that the more particular and concrete the image, the more widely it speaks to more different kinds of people. The preachers we met developed densely textured images that left vivid and lasting impressions so that the image itself became a common experience for all who heard it. Such an image would then also remind hearers of comparable *and* contrary experiences in their own lives. As highly specific points of contact, images permitted a reflective moment in which hearers could ponder how their lives were similar to or different from the preaching image they had just experienced. Like narratives, images are a large-scale speech genre that invites people to complete the sermon in their own lives.

Moving toward rather fine-grained speech genres, we learned the importance of *sayings* within multi-ethnic settings. Studies of oral folklore reveal that those who rely upon oral forms of communication (including highly defined ethnic groups) are more than just quaint storytellers. Their speech repertoire also attends to the littlest bits of language: sayings that permeate everyday life. Some sayings, like proverbs, are tiny gems of wisdom used to instruct and enlighten. Other sayings, like verbal comebacks, are combative devices showing that the speaker sees things differently. Unlike narratives that typically develop toward some eventual resolution, sayings mimic the open-ended struggles of ordinary life and offer highly portable, memorable insights for guidance and redirection.

One preacher we interviewed described how this widespread use of sayings in her own ethnic community also became a staple for preaching in that same place.

> Puerto Ricans and most Hispanics I know have a lot of sayings about things, and many preachers use them. These sayings are very common, a constant part of how people talk, and preachers use them as routine. When a person is preaching and they say those things, everybody knows what they say. But you had to have lived there, or it didn't mean anything. I'm not very good with sayings even though I grew up with them. People use sayings all the time, and I'm always asking what they mean even though I grew up hearing them.

Several insights can be gleaned from this remark. First, the pervasiveness of sayings is a rich opportunity. Sayings can help the preacher quickly connect at a deep level with no need for further explanation. It may well be that a sermon's larger purpose is in fact to challenge the values inherent in a saying, but the ability to do this well depends on the fact that the saying is already widespread. Another preaching opportunity is hinted at through this interviewee's own uncertainty about sayings. A preacher might be able to explore with one ethnic group what a particular saying means, thereby honoring their wisdom while creating a bridge between that group and others. Finally, sayings can render the sermon itself more lasting and available. By being brief and memorable, sayings are meant to be carried into daily life. Sermons that employ them are likely to travel there as well.

One remaining speech genre that was often mentioned by pastors in multiethnic settings was *poetic language*. Operating again at a fairly small scale (like sayings), this genre is more a matter of style and arrangement than of particular content. One interviewee focused the subject in this way:

> The incarnational aspect of the sermon comes out in whether the preacher is articulate. One of the things that I have observed here is a very definite appreciation of preaching as art: how well the sentences come together, the rhetoric, that whole experience. It is "pretty," and there is an aesthetic sense there for somebody who can really work the language. There is a desire for the language to be beautiful and beautifully crafted.

What is intriguing is how this pastor (whose congregation was *not* prone to elite artistic tendencies) portrayed beautifully shaped language as "incarnational" for his hearers. Careful crafting of words is significant because in this way they bear more fully the mystery of God. Of course, the standards for such artistry vary widely from one ethnic group to another, with some valuing elaborate ornamentation and others almost stark simplicity. Sometimes all that is needed to appeal widely across diverse ethnic groups is an intentional use of potent metaphor, memorable alliteration, or pleasing meter. In any case, poetic language that appropriately serves the aims of proclamation is evidently important in many such settings.

Since the four speech genres above indicate the preferred devices of many of those we interviewed, it is not hard on this same basis to deduce forms of speaking they typically avoided. Most felt that proposition-driven or definition-laden approaches typical in earlier generations were not useful in multi-ethnic settings. For similar reasons, expository style was only rarely used, although it did have a limited and focused role in certain ethnic communities. Finally, we were surprised to discern a connection between these preferred genres and the overall tendency by our interviewees to avoid judgmental language. The very genres they urged are at the same time not well suited to open challenge and confrontation. Put another way, their use fits into a larger pattern of using indirect and subtle styles in the language of a sermon.

Engaging Moves

We turn now from speech genres as the building blocks of preaching language to overall strategies for sermon design. The challenge at this general level is not so much how to minimize misunderstanding (as with speech genres) but how to keep an ethnically diverse group of hearers on track during the comprehensive flow of the sermon. Our interviewees offered a handful of related ideas for how the moves of a sermon could build and maintain engagement with hearers.

As a starting point, many preachers we met had abandoned the stock, "one size fits all" sermon designs they once learned. One recalled, "In seminary we used to talk about triads. Now they call it 'problem-point-power' or 'goal-malady-means,' but whatever one of those triads you want to look at, my experience has been that it's like trying to force a round peg in a square hole." Rather than abstract classroom approaches, preachers in multi-ethnic settings were relying more on *correlation* to supply a basic design. The driving move of the sermon correlated an event, insight, or other feature from a biblical text with an experience or even conflict within the ethnic situation of the hearers. The movement was as often from situation to text as it was from text to situation. In either case, this strategy demonstrated what one pastor, alluding to current approaches to scripture translation, called "the principle of dynamic analogy, meaning there are situations that are dynamically analogous to the biblical record." A distinct set of concrete applications derived from this basic correlation might follow next in the sermon, but the correlation itself often was adequate for hearers to connect with their own lives and settings.

Another design strategy for engagement is using moves of *familiarization*. In order for different kinds of ethnic hearers to remain oriented to what is being preached, we were told how important it can be to establish familiar points of contact throughout the span of the sermon. A very common strategy for this was simple repetition: using a phrase as a regular refrain, inviting hearers to say it in unison or to one another, and so forth. This approach has obvious similarities to the use of sayings we mentioned earlier, especially in terms of making the sermon portable and memorable. Beyond this, repetition offers a reassurance for hearers throughout the course of the sermon that they are truly grasping what is being said. So significant is this device that we will hear of its value in several other chapters that follow. We should hasten to note, however, that repetition alone is not enough to provide engagement. One pastor who herself used repetition recalled a time when several of her Latino parishioners attended another church one Sunday and then reported their disappointment with the sermon. "They said to me that he talked thirty minutes and said nothing. So I asked, 'OK, he said *nothing*? What did he preach on?' They said, 'I have no idea. He just went around and around and around, and we heard the same thing he said about four or five times, and he would finish and then he said it again. He spent thirty minutes going around in circles and he said nothing.'" The haunting message in these remarks is that repetition cannot automatically evoke personal connection or sermonic clarity. Instead, it is a strategy by which what is already worthwhile and potentially engaging can be reinforced for our hearers.

Another move to create familiarization in preaching is to employ already familiar elements within the sermon. Instead of creating familiarity as the sermon progresses as with repetition, the preacher relies upon the built-in familiarity of some outside device. Our respondents referred especially to the strategic use of well-known songs and prayers in order to create this kind of reassuring tone in multi-ethnic preaching. We will return to several resources our preachers suggested in this regard later in this chapter.

Given the importance of orality for this cultural frame and others in this book, we learned that *conversation* was a valuable means to create an engaging design. Interviewees often crafted their sermons to progress much like an everyday discussion, with natural moments of give-and-take or question-and-answer. This did not always require, however, an actual dialogue with hearers in which they verbally responded since, for some ethnic groups, to reply audibly would be tasteless or disrespectful. Even so, a casual sermon structure could still create a conversational tone in which hearers participated through interjections and rejoinders supplied solely by the preacher. As often as not, there was no neat conclusion or summary to the structure of these sermons, which instead were left open and unresolved.

Conversational sermon design was seen as especially helpful for addressing two sorts of multi-ethnic preaching challenges. When facing significant difficulties or crises within the congregation, some pastors used the sermon to model a very ethnically familiar way of "talking out" the problem. In this regard, the open-ended nature of this design naturally implied that the conversation would go on once the sermon was finished. Other respondents relied upon conversational design as a simple way of monitoring perceptions during the sermon itself. Unsure or contested meanings could be checked by raising questions to which hearers would reply, thus building stronger engagement.

Since the daily oral repertoire of many ethnic groups is so often rich in stories, it is not surprising that conversational design might include the use of narrative. Although we have mentioned narrative earlier in this chapter as a speech genre, we return to it here as the broad pattern for the entire span of a sermon. While not true for all ethnic groups, of course, some seem to value sermons with an overall story structure, as one pastor in a Native American congregation noted. "The storytelling time here is pretty interactive in that it doesn't just belong to the storyteller. There may be several occasions during that storytelling time when the congregation itself gets involved in the storytelling. That happens by open responses to what is being said at the time, or with an invitation to share a thought or experience that might help embellish that particular story for the day." In such cases, narrative is not a specific moment within a larger framework but instead provides the comprehensive space for an encounter. A sermon so structured creates an engaging world of mutual conversation for all who enter it.

Narrative design reminds us that some ways of arranging sermons work well with only particular ethnic groups. This directs us to another insight from our interviewees that the structure of a sermon at times must attend to matters of *convention*. In our earlier discussion of group characteristics, we noted several expectations that ethnic groups have for the sermon itself. Here we turn to specific conventions of design that different ethnic groups come to expect. Some look for the sermon always to begin with a prayer, which one respondent portrayed as a way by which the congregation became more engaged in opening up the word. Other groups listen for conventional endings in a sermon structure such as songs or closing prayers. Still others regard it as indispensable for sermons to include time for personal testimony from the congregation (although other groups limit this practice to special preaching occasions such as funerals). Of course, none of these conventions serve as generalized guides for sermon design. The point instead is for preachers in multi-ethnic settings to learn the conventional practices that are expected in a particular congregation and use them appropriately as sermonic moves that build engagement.

One final way to think about the engaging moves of a sermon has less to do with overall structure than *presentation*. After all, embodiment and delivery are the basic material means by which preaching makes its appeal, so moves in these areas (literally and figuratively) have a tremendous impact upon how the sermon engages its hearers. Since the "meta-communication" level of delivery (that is, vocal tone and volume, pace of speech, use of body, and so forth) is so subtle, we should not be surprised at the lack of consensus about what forms of presentation might be best in multi-ethnic settings.

The matter is complicated by the fact that our respondents offered conflicting advice about presentation. Some said they "never look at the group directly eye to eye, but sometimes over the heads of the people or simply looking down while speaking," while others said that a lack of eye contact would suggest dishonesty. Some were careful to remain in the pulpit because "the place that the preacher stands is a very sacred and holy place," while others said that they when they spoke amid the assembly "people became excited and said 'He's right down among us.'" Similar disparities included whether the preacher's posture was restrained or emotionally expressive and even whether using written notes created distance from the assembly or conveyed careful study and preparation.

Despite all this variety, there actually were underlying points of commonality that suggest how presentation becomes an important move of engagement. First, the variations we just mentioned all reflected ethnic group standards for strong public speech. While our interviewees could not offer general rules for presentation, their often opposing insights indicate that they attended closely to what particular ethnic groups valued. Not incidentally, many of our respondents had also acquired the flexibility to change cherished modes of presentation for the sake of newly encountered ethnic groups.

Second, our informants consistently affirmed that presentation was not a matter of technique or decoration. At one level, the way a sermon is presented reflects deeply on the pastoral gifts and authority of the preacher. We were told several times that congregations with strong ethnic identities could quickly see through a showy speech to a shallow speaker. At another level, presentation is not only consistent with the pastoral gifts but requires the preacher's effort as well. Matters of delivery were intentionally considered and only rarely left to chance. Those we interviewed gave forethought to when they would change location during the sermon or how the use of body or voice would support sermonic unity. They shared with us the fascinating paradox that it required planning to look natural and greater effort in presentation for the sermon effortlessly to be engaged by hearers.

Artistic Treasures

A basic strategy by which respondents enriched their homiletical language and design was to draw from the artistic treasures of ethnic groups themselves. The broad range of aesthetic forms and practices available through any one ethnic group (let alone many such groups in one congregation) became a main resource for their more focused preaching task of engaging diverse hearers. This broad range about which they spoke does not, however, lead to specific and absolute rules for cross-cultural preaching, since a cherished expression in one ethnic group may evoke indifference or offense in another. What we learned through our interviews, instead, was how to cultivate awareness and use of ethnic artistic treasures that seem to be instructive for anyone in a multi-ethnic situation.

In terms of *awareness of variety*, our interviewees tended to look in several key areas for artistic forms and practices that might have some sort of bearing on preaching. First on most lists was to notice the role of music within ethnic groups. It was often through songs and instruments that some of the deepest levels of ethnic identity were retained and transmitted. A Franciscan priest spoke of how his own order had rediscovered a lesson from centuries earlier, "that music is far more important to the Native people of this continent than the best homilies by our best preachers." For similar reasons, pastors in congregations whose main ethnic group actually consisted of many diverse subgroups described how music was one of the chief markers by which subgroup differences could be identified. Even within a single and fairly unified ethnic group, music might specify social status or caste. One preacher told of how her Vietnamese members resisted collective singing of hymns not because they disliked music, but because singing was a solo event reserved either for priests (temple chanting) or lower-class performers (popular songs). Music is a potent bearer, then, of ethnic memory, identity, and station.

After music, our interviewees looked for kinesthetic ethnic forms such as dance. The wild diversity of dance in different ethnic groups only underscores how this form provides a potent and concentrated embodiment of ethnic identity and values. For the same reason, it was startling how often our informants mentioned times when ethnic dance had been repressed or rejected by church authorities (especially among Native Americans) in order to control and change the religious expressions of these people. As a result, pastors trying to learn more about ethnic dance were often met with skepticism and resistance by ethnic group members themselves. Dance shows how artistic forms and practices can bear not only deep values but open wounds.

Related to dance, ethnic drama was another aesthetic treasure our interviewees tried to explore. We quickly learned from them that the line between theater and other kinds of expression was sometimes difficult to draw. The dances of some Native groups are actually dramatic reenactments of important events, while certain African immigrant groups tell stories that are more of a theatrical performance than an ordinary narrative. Also intriguing in this regard was the rich dramatic heritage of plays and processions found in many different Latino groups, dramas derived from common origins and popular piety. In these cases and more, our informants pointed out the frequency with which dramatic performances carried significant religious themes either implicitly or overtly.

While drama typically occurs in a public setting, our respondents were also on the lookout for private artistic practices such as domestic and family rituals. These are often tied to rites of passage at times like birth, adolescence, marriage, or death. Such occasions are ritually important because of the risk and danger when personal identity is subjected to change or loss. In these very instances, ethnic groups call upon artistic resources to signal a larger cultural home in which life passages can be located and managed. Those we interviewed had come to appreciate how ritual attire, cuisine, instruction, and so forth could be as profoundly expressive as other, more public aesthetic forms.

Besides the range of performances listed above, respondents also naturally considered the ethnic treasure of visual and plastic arts. Although the preachers we met were well aware of these forms, they seemed to play a smaller role in preaching than other ethnic art forms. This may reflect the highly oral and performative orientation of the ethnic groups with which our interviewees dealt, or it may reflect the challenge of using what is static (two- and three-dimensional artifacts) during something active (worship and preaching). We include such forms of expression in this listing, however, because our interviewees were certainly aware of them and, as we will see, sometimes employed them as preaching resources.

Having noted our respondents' awareness of the wide range of ethnic artistic treasures, we turn now to their *patterns of use* within preaching. Preachers tended to employ these forms and practices in two main ways in multi-ethnic settings. One was to draw these into the worship. This involved much more than using art objects to enhance the worship environment, as valuable as those might be. Experienced cross-cultural preachers were especially intent on using performances as a part of worship, both to honor the ethnic groups involved and to serve as a reference point during the preaching.

For example, a pastor in a congregation with many Laotian members arranged for a traditional dance from that group during the offering time. Using bodily postures as "an expression of celebrating who we are as a gift from God and a gift back to God," the dance became a focal element in the ensuing sermon on offering. In a similar way, a worship service on Holy Saturday was enhanced by including Filipino dancers at a key point in the liturgy, as the priest explained: "There is a graceful dance of the young women, a very graceful dance with two lanterns, one in each hand, but sometimes with one balancing on the head. And we incorporated that into our Easter Vigil celebration, a very slow-moving dance that brings the light in at the time of the procession of the paschal candle. And for them, this touches some of the roots of their culture." Such vivid imagery and movement was then naturally incorporated into the homily. It is not difficult to imagine many other ways that ethnically specific forms and practices employed in the course of worship could also be resources for preaching.

The other way our interviewees used ethnic artistic treasures was within the sermon itself. Rather than referring to something in the larger worship, this approach

calls for rethinking the sermon's design at a fundamental level. We have already alluded to preaching in which music not only augments the sermon but also provides its structure, as with the periodic singing of a refrain or series of verses. The
use of drama as the central preaching event was also frequently suggested as a way
to reenact a biblical text. We even heard of several cases where artwork or a cultural artifact became the focus of extensive examination during the sermon. The
pastor of a church with many immigrant Chinese members mentioned this example: "I start by writing a Chinese character out. Let me give an example: 'boat'
in Chinese is one *sampan* with eight people sitting there. Eight people—so you ask
the Chinese how come there are only eight people sitting there. How come not
nine, not six? Because in the Bible, it is the very first boat: the ark, Noah's ark, with
eight people." Preachers emphasized that their aim was not to pander to an ethnic
group and its treasures. Instead, artistic elements served as a way of connecting
the ethnic group to the heart of the biblical proclamation. Another intent in using
aesthetic materials in this way was to enrich the worldview of all the congregants.
After all, most of our interviewees were preaching in *multi*-ethnic settings. One
group's artistic resources were chosen not to the exclusion of others but instead to
broaden the perspective of the entire gathering. Such a strategy also prompted
other ethnic groups to seek their own points of connection with the sermon and
the biblical text.

Active Texts

The varied denominations of our interviewees were reflected in quite different
ways of choosing sermon texts, from so-called "free text" approaches to reliance
upon a lectionary. Even so, these preachers seemed to be even more concerned
about what a text did than what it said, its activity rather than strictly its substance. Content was not ignored, of course, but texts were used in sermons less for
their ideas and concepts than their events and encounters. In particular, those
with experience in multi-ethnic settings gravitated toward two important strategies in using biblical texts.

On the one hand, many of our interviewees sought out texts that most ably
created a *worldview*. This meant, as many readers may have guessed, a tendency to
lean on biblical narratives. Respondents drew heavily from the Old Testament because of the especially vivid portrayals there of sorrow, conflict, exile, and faithfulness (or the lack thereof). Such narratives became a place for ethnic hearers to
encounter struggles comparable to their own. Another frequently used and perhaps surprising literary genre was wisdom literature. Proverbs that provided
guidance or psalms that offered expressive language for prayer also activated their
own distinctive worldview. These texts were not used as ideas to be analyzed but
instead presented hearers a range of emotions to which God is attentive and a
path for living on which God is the guide.

On the other hand, our respondents learned to look for biblical texts that most ably claimed a *perspective*, especially one attuned to the experiences of particular ethnic groups. Texts that dealt with struggles for power or longings for justice were regularly visited. Even allegedly sterile epistolary texts became useful insofar as they conveyed real community conflict comparable to something being experienced today. Such perspectival strategies both valued contemporary ethnic challenges and placed these within a larger framework of God's healing and hope. One of our respondents nicely summarized this by noting, "It's through those stories, those texts of scripture that all of us have our lives." Overall, then, this strategy of seeking active texts is less a question of which parts of scripture to select than how any particular texts are used. In multi-ethnic settings, reading scripture for its worldviews and perspectives seems to matter most.

3. The Frame of Class

Faith Church was a mirror of its college-town setting. In many ways, its members simply reflected the classic "town-gown" spread felt in the larger community. Some were locals from rural or blue-collar roots who were long-term survivors from tough times and now enjoyed a measure of prosperity. Others were newcomers with university positions whose careers had already carried them to various parts of the country. Beneath the differences, however, were profound similarities. Both newcomers and locals valued family stability, formal education, church involvement, and a broad array of resources to which they could turn in times of trouble.

As their pastor, JoAnn bore those same differences and similarities in her personal background. Like the locals, her farm family had known hardship and demanding physical work, but like the newcomers, her professional training put her at ease with rapid change and high-powered campus settings. Like all the members of her congregation, moreover, she had known the benefits of family, education, church, and resources. As her tenure went on, however, she also came to recognize a segment in their larger community to which none of them in the church bore much resemblance.

In the common and unkind parlance of the community, this segment was known as "trailer trash" or "low-rent losers." Seldom attaining beyond a high school degree, many of these people regarded formal education with contempt. Under a single roof one might find a complex, multigenerational blend of divorce, remarriage, long-term unmarried partners, and children from various sets of parents. Physical, emotional, and substance abuse were routine, producing a persistent mood of crisis. Income came through a patchwork of low-paying jobs on unpopular shifts in factories or service occupations, typically with few or no benefits. Above all, a "respectable" place like Faith Church had never been part of their labored lives.

Increasingly, however, JoAnn was finding herself not simply meeting this segment of the community, but even being identified by some of them as "our pastor." The route to her first meeting with many of them was often the same: tragedy. One typical contact came when the local funeral director called on her to preside at the burial of a middle-aged man who had suffered a lengthy bout with cancer. Having lost his job at a nearby meat-packing plant when it went bankrupt, this man and his family scraped together what little money they could from various service-sector jobs to pay for his medical treatment. JoAnn had never met the extended family prior to the brief graveside service, and she was sure their paths would never cross again. A year later, though, when the widow's only son was crushed by a car at a drag race, her instruction to the funeral director was simply, "Call our pastor." That was JoAnn.

JoAnn was baffled by these newfound relationships. How were such obvious class differences being bridged? How could she minister among these people so that comfort or hope might be heard? Whatever the answers, however, one thing was clear: JoAnn's preaching was already getting through. Recalling another funeral, this time of a local junkyard operator, she contrasted two very different kinds of proclamation:

> I was one of two pastors asked to do the funeral. The other pastor was this hunting buddy who had spent a great deal of time trying to convert the father [the junkyard operator] to his own brand of fundamentalism. The family asked me to preach and the other pastor to offer a eulogy. Well, the other pastor used his "eulogy" to speak of sin and damnation, to question our eternal status, and to offer an altar call. My homily, which followed his testimonial, was calm, scriptural, and, I think, hopeful. Naively, I assumed that his theological approach made more sense to the family than mine. After all, aren't these people really fundamentalists at heart? Instead, the family thanked me profusely for my kind words and faithful care while hardly acknowledging the other pastor's words at all.

JoAnn did not gloat over the outcome but instead was genuinely perplexed by this turn of events. What did it matter that she did everything right if she had no idea why?

JoAnn's ability to reach those so dramatically different from herself, however, was not as mysterious as it might seem. First, there was a distinctive *situation* involved in many of these encounters. Simply put, JoAnn met people at the point of their deepest needs. Rather than expecting others to conform to a predefined view of the faith, she came to them in the face of difficulty and even tragedy and thereby built the basis for ongoing pastoral contact. Second, it was significant in the incident above how the family recognized that a caring *relationship* had been established. They could hear what JoAnn had to say as a preacher because she had first been with them as their pastor. As we have said several times before, what happens outside the pulpit is often the most important factor in creating effective cross-cultural preaching. Finally, the *resources* that one group may take for granted can, at times, have a potent impact upon those who have never heard them before. For those wearied by a tiresome and predictable cant of judgmentalism, the grace and hope central to JoAnn's theological tradition and therefore to her preaching was a surprising and liberating alternative.

Our task in this chapter is to discuss the available alternatives for preachers who take seriously the cultural frame of *class*. In everyday life, of course, class is thoroughly enmeshed with the cultural realities of ethnicity, displacement, and beliefs. For our purposes here, however, it is important to notice what class distinctively can disclose, again organizing our interview responses into remarks about *group characteristics* and *preaching strategies*. In preparation for that, we must first revisit the typical view in which class serves merely as a synonym for economic status. What might be lost about a broader experience of class because of this simplistic equation?

Class and Status

Some form of social hierarchy is customary in virtually every human group. The difference comes in how such hierarchies have been ordered. For much of the history of the premodern West as well as various parts of the world yet today, hierarchy was ordered along various social criteria. It was possible to tell where a person belonged in the larger social scheme on the basis of family descent, public prestige, personal character, and the like. For this reason, enormous attention was paid to such topics as lineage, honor, and virtue in order to determine an individual's rank in relation to others. Since these realities were relatively fixed (for example, one's parentage obviously could not be changed), social place was simply a given. The order of society thus had a natural, taken-for-granted quality that could be neither denied nor defied.

With the massive social changes that accompanied Western industrial and political revolutions in the eighteenth century, these social criteria for hierarchy began to lose their meaning. By the advent of the nineteenth century, such hierarchy began to be presented in economic categories instead. The widespread use of "class" to speak of an economically oriented hierarchy is, therefore, of very recent origin, and represented a substitution for the previously more familiar language of "station," "rank," or "privilege," which were based on social criteria.

In basic terms, social theorists starting in the nineteenth century distinguished upper classes by their ownership of capital and control of the labor and production of others. Lower classes, by contrast, were subservient to such control and dependent upon wages for their economic well-being. Middle classes, a new urban phenomena emerging in early modern Europe, had relative economic autonomy but lacked the degree of control and ownership known among the upper classes. Rather than focus on the adequacy of this analysis, it is valuable for us simply to recognize that the criteria for hierarchy underwent a dramatic shift away from the social and toward the economic. With this shift came the perceived possibility that one's place in the social order could change. Either by individual effort (success or failure) or by class conflict (revolutionary overthrow), a person might attain a different social place.

In its linguistic origins, class also has a deeply economic quality. It comes from the Latin *classis*, which itself had a military derivation and referred to a fleet that had been called together (from the Greek *kaleo*, "to call"). In the sixth century B.C.E., however, the word was transformed to speak of the economic value of the different divisions in Roman society. Within this framework, *classicus* referred to that Roman class with the greatest economic value, *the* class above which no other existed. These etymological features still bear upon on how class is understood today. From its military roots, class conveys the sense of an imposed grouping called into being by external forces. From its social use, class conveys the sense of a divided reality, much as when we "classify" as a means for analysis and control. From its ordering quality, class conveys the sense of a value-laden hierarchy, similar to when we refer to great works of art as being "classic." Class as imposed, divisive, and evaluative affects the way it is internalized today as a cultural frame and therefore has an enormous potential impact upon preaching.

It is this internalization of the frame of class to which we want to give special attention. Ironically, what can become lost in the strictly economic view of class is the premodern awareness of social criteria in hierarchy. Although an economic sense of class remains basic, this must be expanded to include how economic reality affects the social contours of identity, prestige, authority, capacity, and so forth. On the one hand, an adequate view of class must account for how it contributes to the perception of a self-perpetuating, self-fulfilling social hierarchy. This hierarchy seems to have a durability with which people must contend even when their economic circumstances have radically changed. On the other hand, an adequate view of class must allow for a certain amount of social fluidity. Unlike older notions of rank or station, class is not static and closed but dynamic and open. A single class may well incorporate complicated, internal tensions (due to ethnicity, education, family, etc.) while allowing at the same time for alliances with those of other classes.

In order to provide this more adequate view of class, we propose treating it less as an external category for social analysis than as an internalized experience that is deeply felt. As a result, it is a powerful cultural frame through which we see ourselves and others. More specifically, this internalized experience appears to be felt by all of us in at least five different ways regardless of which class we might claim for ourselves. Though not exhaustive, these can be envisioned as a series of interrelated layers that may suggest still others. Beyond this, readers will likely sense a markedly religious quality to the values embedded in these many layers. Paying attention to this in particular will enrich our awareness of the deeply theological dimensions of class, an especially important consideration in cross-cultural preaching.

One of the central outcomes of class is that everyone, regardless of class, is subjected to a framework of comparison. Those in different classes do not occupy different worlds but instead learn a common system of assessment by which personal value and validation may be garnered or withheld. Therefore, the first way in which the experience of class is internalized is through a basic sense of human *worth*. By looking within and beyond our class situation, we are schooled in what attains dignity and respect as well as what prevents shame and failure. Although the impetus for this scrutiny initially is economic, class identity eventually pervades the sense of worth at a psychological and moral level as well. Diminished worth imposed on lower classes can create self-doubt that endures even when economic fortunes improve, while elevated worth imputed to middle or upper classes can evoke self-confidence that promotes dignity (or, in some cases, denial) when fortunes plummet.

This scrutiny of comparative worth encouraged by class awareness has as its by-product a heightened sensitivity to the order of things. Knowing the rules of how things are supposed to work means that a sense of *justice* becomes internalized at all class levels. This sort of justice, however, is rigid and relentless. Since class represents an allegedly orderly and rational hierarchy, it promotes a worldview governed by strict balance and causality. Every effort produces an equivalent outcome so that people get only and exactly what they deserve. At each class level, this leads on the one hand to an attitude of entitlement (having a right to what one has) and on the other to an attitude of isolation (having only oneself to blame). The irony is that, far from promoting dissatisfaction, this sense of justice can actually reinforce class identity so that the system itself is defended. Instead of questioning the hierarchical assumptions of class, the greater concern is to root out any unfairness that might lead to imbalance and eventual chaos. This is why we sometimes can notice intraclass pressure toward conformity, discouraging a level of education, choice of spouse, or type of attire that seems not to fit within the equitable and orderly perception of a given class.

Since control of the means of production is basic to a modern view of class, it is to be expected that a certain sense of *labor* will be internalized through this frame. Indeed, labor is bound up with what we have already said about human worth. Simply put, who you are becomes a question of what you do, so that demonstrated ability counts more than abstract essence. This means, in the first place, that labor is seen in terms of capacity. Work is more valuable depending on the amount achieved, with the corollary that personal dignity supposedly can be enhanced through greater effort. Conversely, disability or inactivity become ways of judging others negatively (through labels like "handicapped" or "lazy poor," for example). In the second place, labor is seen in terms of mastery. Work is more valuable if it is not generic and replaceable but offers some distinctive skill or produces some social benefit. Upper classes in particular view labor as specific tasks tied to distinct roles rather than as general exertion. Finally, labor is seen in terms of authority. Work is more valuable depending upon the power to control what is done. Some persons are legitimated to give the orders that others are simply obligated to obey. Especially in lower classes, the result can be a passive and deferential attitude toward authority figures coupled with the effort to wield personal power through low-level strategies of resistance, like foot-dragging or sabotage on the job. All told, then, the frame of class refocuses the way we see ourselves through basic labor questions of how much, what kind, and who says.

The foregoing has serious implications for the ways people feel attached to others in society. Perceptions about human dignity, fair treatment, and valued effort have a potent impact upon the sense of *loyalty* in belonging to groups. Those with economic privileges naturally treat society in general and groups in particular as trustworthy and beneficial. Voluntary organizations such as churches are places to receive support, reinforce attitudes, express concerns, and forge connections. By contrast, the economically vulnerable are more familiar with being marginalized from such belonging and even treated with suspicion or disdain. While this reinforces the indignity that class can evoke, it also awakens the perceived injustice of exclusionary treatment. Those alienated from "respectable" groups see them as hypocritical and inconsistent with their own goals. As a result, those on the margins of society end up with a marginal interest in belonging. What other class levels might view as erratic and uncommitted participation is, however, the very selective loyalty reserved in lower classes only for those who are already proven to be trustworthy, like family and friends. Many voluntary groups, by contrast, elicit from these same people a more circumspect participation on an as-needed basis rather than a deep commitment to group ideas and values.

Finally, class can help us recognize the sense of *voice* people have internalized for purposes of self-expression. For example, those with authority over their own labor and that of others utter commands that are then followed. Such people function in a reality where thoughts become actions and ideas bring results. Beyond this, knowing is not just a basis for doing but also for belonging. That is, such people tend to join those groups whose ideals they share. By contrast, those in other class situations view cognitive knowledge and rational reflection rather differently. Their thoughts and ideas have typically been ignored or, worse still, used to shame them. As a result, they look elsewhere to express themselves in emotional and bodily forms. Whatever one strongly feels or vividly experiences is what counts, even though to outsiders it might seem irrational and intolerant. In a related way, Tex Sample has noted the class distinction between those who view faith in God as an object of understanding as opposed to those who treat it as a focus for believing. Class is the basis for these different kinds of religious voice.

We have argued that a more adequate view of the frame of class would include the internalized and interrelated levels of worth, justice, labor, loyalty, and voice. These five contribute to the particular and complex class identity and worldview we each carry within. By noticing them, we can recognize our vast cultural differences without losing sight of the fundamental similarity across all classes in being shaped by the ideologies of this system. Understood in this way, class becomes a significant consideration for the cross-cultural preacher, and we look now to our interviews to see its impact upon the task of preaching.

Group Characteristics

Although class is an internalized cultural reality, that of course does not render it private. Like ethnicity, class can involve shared experiences and worldviews that are quite potent. Unlike ethnicity, however, the sense of mutual commitment within a class often remains relatively low. People are not overtly taught to be middle class in the same way that they might learn their Polish heritage. At the same time, to be seen as part of a class is, by its very nature, to be embedded in a comparative, socially reinforced hierarchy. Class exemplifies what the anthropologist Mary Douglas called "high grid, low group": placement within a social structure, but with only a minimal sense of belonging. If this portrays the general terrain of class, our interviews revealed four group characteristics that place its contours in sharper relief: multiple identity, ambiguous authority, thought process, and symbolic burden. Seeing the significance of each helps preachers more accurately navigate through the distinctive landscape of class.

Multiple Identity

The ability to notice different classes at all is arguably a more complicated task than with ethnic groups. In the first place, basic unwillingness to see things as they are contributes to a kind of blindness. Especially at the poorest end of the spectrum we may deny the obvious, so that class remains *hidden*. One pastor spoke of this in the exurban congregation he served, echoing a theme we heard often. "It may be the poverty here is a different poverty or we have a different sense of poverty. But it's really a sense of recognizing the poor. The poor are in our midst, but they're really out of sight, and maybe we lose touch with poverty. The food pantry brings a few in, but that's it." The simple fact that persons in one class are invisible to those in another already suggests an important way class shapes group identity. When part of society can be erased from view, members of all classes learn and reinforce basic lessons about personal dignity and social power.

Even with eyes wide open, however, class distinctions can be *subtle* and hard
to spot. A preacher who moved from a multi-ethnic suburban congregation to
a largely Anglo lower-middle-class church in another city remarked about this
difficulty.

> Unlike crossing the racial barrier of going into an African American congregation
> or a Hispanic congregation where it's really clear to you that you have entered an-
> other culture, it's less obvious when the line is a class line. I think it becomes ob-
> vious pretty fast, but the ability to identify and reflect upon the ways in which
> everything has changed, well, it's a more subtle kind of thing. I was much less
> aware of the attitudes I had there than I needed to be.

In this case, the issue was not one of denial but unawareness. Note, however, that
two things eventually did become clear to this pastor: both the public signals of
class difference and a private disposition toward those differences. This particular
interviewee went on to speak at great length of how an increased sophistication in
learning to see class had led to an increased discomfort with long-held personal
values.

Part of what makes class identity so subtle is that, as we have noted before,
there is more at stake than just economic status. Our interviewees usually referred
to a highly *complex* identity further shaped by several noneconomic factors. They
commented, for example, that a person's financial or vocational situation might
accurately indicate only present or recent class while failing to reflect a longer trajectory of enriching or degrading life experiences. Somewhat related was the impact of education, as one pastor in downtown San Francisco contributed.

> A key factor in this thing of socioeconomic level, it seems to me, is the educational
> level of the person. We have some folks who are low income but have a high degree
> of education. And actually we have a few who have a very good income but don't
> have much education. That factor would seem to be almost as critical, or even as
> critical, as how much a person might earn or whether they are employed or not.
> One of our wealthiest members was laid off and unemployed for three years, and he
> was looking for work—looking hard. We all knew he had no income at all. But he's
> a fellow who is quite educated and therefore would tend to have different sorts of
> expectations from a person that was not so educated but might have more income.

Beyond life experience and education, interviewees said that class became complex when intermingled with ethnicity. A pastor of a congregation originally established for Korean immigrants but now quite ethnically varied described her
situation.

> Economic issues stand in real tension, not just in relation to the Korean population
> but in the whole picture of this congregation. There tends to be some hierarchy of

economics, just like society tends to do with the lightening or darkening of the skin. The members that are Hispanic really do come from a harder economic struggle. The Korean people we have tend to be a step above. They also tend to work an awful lot, and that's where a lot of their economic stability has come from. Then our Anglo members tend to be seniors who are fairly comfortable. So when in that multicultural context you overlay the economic issues, it really impacts people very differently, and it takes some sensitivity to address those issues.

Class therefore produces a complex identity both because several factors comprise it and because it interacts with other culture-shaping factors.

Even when adhering more strictly to economic aspects, those we interviewed portrayed dramatically *diverse* class identities within congregations. Part of that diversity resulted, of course, from wide income differences within a single community, placing strains on a congregation's integrity and unity. A preacher in San Jose remarked:

The staggering reality is that in one of the wealthiest areas in the United States, Silicon Valley, 40 percent of the children live below the poverty line. The most challenging aspect of our county is the rich are getting richer and the rest are becoming poorer. And a lot of the people in these communities are immigrant or indigenous, and their children are in that category below the poverty line. The challenge of being at [this church] is that those in the upper middle class are worshiping and working side by side with people who are in the lower economic group. The parish in its forty years has always had a deep commitment to social change and transformation. So I have to periodically remind people of the conditions.

Sometimes, however, class diversity may be periodic rather than ongoing. An influx of migrant labor might produce sharp economic contrasts for only a season. In another case, tourism might make the difference. A pastor whose parish is on an island spoke of two economic communities: the year-round residents who "just eke by" on what they earn during the tourist season and the summer population with "half-million-dollar 'cottages' that no winter resident could ever have."

Diversity can also be evident within a single class. A pastor who served in several small rural communities knew that many of his church members were undeniably poor. As for the Native Americans in those same congregations, however, he added, "When I'm speaking to Native people in [these towns], these are the poor of the poor, way beyond poverty level. Jesus says, 'Blessed are the poor,' but what in the world that means to those people is different than what it means to the rest." Naturally, the same may be true at the other end of the economic spectrum when many are well off, but some seem unimaginably so.

By speaking of class as hidden, subtle, complex, and diverse, our respondents clarified that it is not a singular reality. Just as ethnicity is characterized by subgroup tensions, so also class is characterized by multiple identity. This multiple identity implies, in turn, different expectations about church and scripture of which the preacher should be aware. For example, we heard of cases where the tangled class factors of income, life experience, and education led to hopes by poorer members for the church to be a vehicle for social betterment. Any effort to simplify the worship supposedly to appeal to these same persons in fact ran afoul of their complex expectations. On the other hand, pastors in congregations with significant class differences especially felt that they would be expected by their hearers to speak to economic issues that arose within the Sunday readings. "If you read the text," said one preacher, "and the question is there in the text, then you've got to address it in a way that is of comfort to the people."

How can the preacher anticipate these expectations? Many respondents offered a simple piece of advice.

> I've got a Wednesday morning Bible study group at the church that includes about a dozen people. I'd say a third of them are unemployed or unemployable, another third are largely employed, and the other third are pretty well educated and independent. Working with them is a kind of freewheeling discussion that I certainly don't lead as the scholar in residence or even the local authority. It's taken us years to get to this, but people who came into that group three or four years ago who had never opened scripture now are reading and jumping right into the congregation, challenging things, speaking directly out of their own personal experience. That has become a key part of my understanding of how to work with scripture, because it's a slice of the congregation with which I can interact about the very thing I will be preaching.

Assembling a text study group with people from different classes was often endorsed as a way to increase awareness and improve the way preaching could reach all members. As the quote above also suggests, this holds the further potential to empower those same participants.

Ambiguous Authority

Earlier in this chapter we sketched five interrelated areas in which the effects of class are felt: worth, justice, labor, loyalty, and voice. Permeating that discussion were matters of *personal authority* that affect basic questions like whose word counts, which work matters, and why people gather. Authority profoundly influences how people from different classes speak, act, and belong. Naturally, then, it also affects the way people listen to others, and for this reason preachers need fully to be aware of how authority is perceived. When it comes to the frame of class, however, the topic is decidedly ambiguous.

Interviewees in mixed-class congregations reported that more economically well-off members tended to view personal authority as beneficial. This is understandable since such people are often also in a position to exert some measure of that authority themselves. To be sure, these same persons will respect the authority of others only when it has been earned and does not interfere with their own autonomy. While this creates an innate level of suspicion about personal authority as something to be guarded and not conferred lightly, even so the overall outlook remains basically positive.

When speaking of lower-class or economically destitute members, however, these same preachers pointed out the broadly negative view of personal authority that held sway. This is not only because poorer persons wield little authority of their own, but also because their encounters with authority figures have so frequently been harmful. One pastor remarked: "I think probably one of the challenges even with using our words is that within many of the positions that [poorer members] hold, authority has usually been something used against them, used to keep them down. One of the challenges for me as a preacher is not to buy into what has become for them a very stereotypical view of authority that becomes one of patronage or 'power over.'" Worse still, the central focus for such persons often becomes, as one respondent put it, "scrapping for a livelihood and fighting really hard to get to a place where you feel like you're even a little bit secure economically." When stability is difficult to attain and harder still to preserve, then the authority of others can easily be seen as a threat.

Although broad, this typology of reactions is nonetheless significant when we turn to the *pastoral authority* of preachers. Those we interviewed recognized how their own ability to act and speak as pastors was shaped by class perceptions of personal authority. One person offered this contrast: "When I was in congregations where there were lots of white-collar folks making good money and having power of their own, I was just another person. You know, I functioned for pastoral care—and that was important. But when I've been in congregations where the people are lower on the economic ladder, there's more need to hear hope, and the pastor is the one who carries the authority to announce it." These remarks also suggest the irony that those most likely to have been harmed by others may also, because of their plight, be most open to pastoral authority rightly exercised. By the same token, when ministerial conduct ends up reinforcing negative class reactions to authority, the results can be devastating. One pastor spoke of how difficult it had been to follow a string of pastors who abused and neglected her predominantly working class congregation in the past. Left "spiritually malnourished and unable for a long time to be the church they wanted to be," they were only now beginning to turn a corner in trusting her.

Given these realities about class, then, pastoral authority cannot be presumed. In ways quite consistent with chapter 2, our respondents made patient, intentional efforts to establish appropriate pastoral authority. At first, this called for simple reassurances of competency: knowing your tasks and doing them reliably. This basic move strongly enhanced how pastoral authority was perceived across all classes. Building on this, our informants then tried to convey special commitment to the congregation and its community. Noticing what truly mattered in a particular place over the long run tended to deflate power struggles at the upper end of the social spectrum and cleared a space for direct intervention at the other. Finally, those we interviewed established pastoral authority by means of caring relationships. One pastor we met spoke of his journey this way:

> I think that at first the authority given to me was fairly minimal, sort of *pro forma*. But now, I'm their pastor. By virtue of what I know about them and what I've shared with them, by virtue of how they know me and what they've shared with me, by virtue of what we've done together and who we've become together, in other words, by virtue of the pastor/people relationship, they have increasingly granted me more authority as a preacher. They have sensed that I deeply and genuinely care for them, and they for me.

Building pastoral authority by showing competency, commitment, and caring is thus a process, and one that cannot be rushed.

Just as pastoral authority is influenced by different class perceptions of personal authority, so it can also be affected by how a class regards *scriptural authority*. Readers of this book are no doubt aware that sociological research has shown a correlation between class factors of income and education and views of scriptural authority. This was also quite evident in our conversations with pastors.

> Those who have lower educational levels here would tend to give more authority to scripture without critically viewing it. Those with higher education, with more social standing and more economic means, would tend to place less authority on scripture because of the way they critically approach it. They would ask questions of scripture, disagree with it or argue with it, and would have no problem doing that. They would still say that the Bible has authority for them, but in more of a thematic way, whereas folks with a lower educational or socioeconomic level would tend to take a more "proof text" view of scripture.

What these remarks actually suggest is not that scripture has a lower or higher authority along class lines, but rather that how it functions as an authority varies by class. Some informants worried about tendencies toward literalistic use of the Bible among lower classes. Regardless of use, however, interviewees stressed that scripture itself was highly respected across all class lines, holding an authority that must be acknowledged.

In light of this, scriptural authority came to be seen as a further way for building appropriate pastoral authority. Just as we saw with various ethnic groups, pastors were more able to be respected in mixed class situations to the degree they rooted their actions and ultimately their preaching in scripture itself. This did not require adopting one particular interpretive framework, but taking the

Bible seriously as authoritative within the congregation and thus for its pastor as well. Setting aside all other interpretive questions, one pastor remarked, "When you are preaching to [all these classes], you must somehow just make the connection between the text and what is happening in life. *Then* it has authority." Pastoral authority is enhanced by scriptural authority when pastors try to forge just such a connection.

Thought Process

The foregoing remarks on authority could be read in yet another way. Although we emphasized what they show about the topic itself (authority holds an ambiguous place in different classes), they also reveal subjective reactions to that topic (class experience shapes different ways of thinking). Seen this way, reactions to authority can be seen as but one instance of how reasoning in general is influenced by class. Our interviewees noticed such basic patterns of reasoning and spoke of how these had a significant bearing upon their ministry and preaching. It is to these overall patterns and thought processes shaped by class experience that we now turn.

Of course, it is not terribly fruitful to speak of such patterns in the abstract. It is only when people think *about* something that we in turn can reflect on their thought processes as such. As it turns out, however, one of our interviews provided just such a specific instance, and on a subject dear to readers of this book: preaching. The pastor of a venerable Presbyterian congregation in a major downtown setting described how class experiences intersected with what his hearers expected from his sermons. His comments are quite revealing not simply about preaching, therefore, but about thought processes as well. We reproduce here a lengthy extract from that interview that not only names the basic contrast he saw but also provides a good deal for us to reflect upon later. Speaking about different views of the sermon itself, the pastor began:

> It's a very complex congregation to preach to. It's a challenge every Sunday because there are highly educated people, and they tend to have expectations of the preacher that there would occasionally be quotes, oh, from the *New York Times* or from the latest bestsellers or the latest theological tomes coming out on the market. And they expect their preacher to be reading those and occasionally using them in the sermon. Coupled with that is the expectation of those that have very little education and therefore low expectations of what might be considered more classical Presbyterian-style preaching—highly organized and intellectually designed sermons.

He then continued his remarks by moving outward to the relation between the sermon and the larger flow of worship.

I get the feeling that for folks on a higher socioeconomic level, the way a sermon might tie in with all the other parts of worship might be more important to them or have more significance for them, would heighten their experience of worship. It isn't often, for example, that a poorer person in our congregation would come up to me afterwards and say, "Wow, the sermon, the prayers, and the hymns really seemed to work together to make this a powerful experience." On the other hand, for one of our lawyers or editors, highly educated persons, it is quite common for them to note how the sermon thematically fits well or, in some cases, didn't fit well. They tend more naturally to look at the sermon as part of a whole, whereas folks who have less education and are on a lower socioeconomic level might see the sermon as almost a detachable part. It's just such a different expression in worship, different from any other thing. It's done by one person. It's done for a sustained period of time. It's very personal and intimate, quite different from singing a hymn together with other congregants or listening to a prayer that is directed to God. The sermon is directed really to them. So I think they would tend to view the sermon as kind of a unique event out of the whole worship.

While readers may wish to challenge particular parts of this pastor's conclusions, his remarks were quite consistent with the wide range of others interviewed. Preachers experienced with mixed class congregations typically spoke of a similar kind of divide in what their members listened for in preaching.

The issue before us is what these particular attitudes toward preaching show us more generally about thought process as a group characteristic of class. Recalling that class identity consists of multiple factors, we can initially discern two very different *streams of reasoning* that correspond with class differences. Those with higher formal education, greater economic resources, or broader life experiences are more likely to value forms of thinking that privilege consistency and deductive orderliness. Life is seen in holistic terms, and thus logics that interconnect and contribute to patterns of the whole are more highly prized. In a related way, the quotation above alluded to high expectations of thematic unity and integration of elements, both within and beyond the sermon.

By contrast, those at the opposite end of the class spectrum apparently have less use for such ways of thinking. Some of our interviewees speculated that, because the lives of many lower-class and poor persons are so much on the edge and so frequently in crisis, their very mode of existence requires a more tactical and pragmatic approach. Commonsense thinking to achieve specific ends is finally what counts. As a result, thinking itself is more episodic and less concerned with overall continuity. This does not mean utter mental chaos, however. In fact, several respondents pointed to a different kind of guiding logic: a narrative way of reasoning. Distinct events or issues matter insofar as they are embedded in a larger story that gives them purpose. In any case, the stream of reasoning in such cases is less concerned with what fits a pattern than what enables an outcome.

Related to these distinctive streams, we can also discern two different *warrants for reasoning*. A "warrant" is simply what any reasoning leans on to support why it should be accepted by others. Whenever we want our thoughts or actions to be taken seriously, we look for some kind of backing to lend credibility and strength. That backing is a warrant. It is not hard to imagine how warrants for reasoning might in turn relate to a preferred stream of reasoning. We already noted that, among those whose economic security is tenuous or academic attainment is modest, reasoning tends to be focused on outcomes. Such thinking is usually best warranted by appeals to concrete situations, personal experiences, and effective practices. This is why, in the extensive quote above, the poorer members valued a personal orientation in preaching. Other interviews revealed a comparable preference for the use of concrete examples. If hearers recognize a connection to their lives and settings, it is more likely to help them meet real needs or face specific challenges. Concretely grounded warrants are therefore most likely to further the narrative of otherwise episodic lives.

When the preacher in the example above referred to the upper and professional classes in the congregation, of course, a very different set of warrants came into play. For these people, appealing to sources (such as recent publications) and effectively using ideas (by creating intellectual patterns and structures) were much more important. This is only to be expected, since such warrants better contribute to a stream of reasoning oriented to consistent, deductive logic. At this end of the class spectrum, abstractness and reflection displace concreteness and outcomes as the chief warrants for reasoning.

We wish to emphasize, however, that none of this discussion implies stronger or weaker abilities to reason based on class situation. Our interviewees were being descriptive rather than evaluative in commenting on how class influences thinking. In fact, there was deep appreciation for the way different thought processes are quite well suited to the special needs and demands of particular class situations. In any case, these different streams of and warrants for reasoning explain more fully why in mixed class settings, a single sermon can have such variable significance, or with certain hearers even fail to connect.

Symbolic Burden

The frame of class reveals one last group characteristic for cross-cultural preachers to consider. Our informants pointed out several common values that matter across a wide range of class experiences. In a positive sense, these are basic goals for human striving. When attained, they symbolize blessing and even privilege. More hauntingly, though, these same values are fragile and difficult for some people to preserve. When unattained, they instead symbolize failure and even worthlessness. These symbolic values therefore bear a double burden, both as focus for achievement and, at the other extreme, reminder of deficiency. Since lower classes often know only the second of these symbolic burdens, those we interviewed gave them special attention in the remarks that follow.

As a starting point, we heard about the symbolics of *order*. People in comfortable circumstances are able to assume a level of personal wholeness and social concord that operates as a baseline for all other matters of living. According to our interviewees, however, such stability for lower classes was constantly under assault on many fronts in what sounded like a kind of experiential warfare. One pastor commented:

> Some of the people are dealing with some of the inequities they face: bosses that don't care and positions where they know they can be replaced very easily. There are also questions of self-worth. The issue isn't so much "Why me?" but more "This is what we deserve." And then there really is a tendency toward hopelessness. Most of them are not one paycheck away from poverty but probably not more than two. They face some really challenging economic realities. There are challenging emotional realities within some of the families as well. They've tried to raise their kids well, but some major difficulties have happened.

Although these comments gesture ahead to other symbolic burdens we will mention below, at this point it is simply worthwhile to notice the range of assaults from a number of different angles. In terms of work, individual self, finances, family, and more besides, order is replaced by disarray.

The impression, then, is of lives that are profoundly fragmented rather than integrated and whole. This fragmentation is symbolized in one further way, as another pastor noted. "I am very aware, when I step in the pulpit, of the disparity of lifestyle and of economic resources in [this congregation], held in this one body of people. I am aware of the resentments. I am aware of the prejudice on both parts, what they believe about one another." Note the reciprocal nature of these resentments, all of which are actually centered on the symbol of order. For those whose lives are already under assault, bitterness is directed against those who represent an order that remains, for themselves, beyond reach. From the opposite perspective, however, resentment can be equally pronounced. Those with fragmented lives represent a disruption in ordered life that might happen to anyone, a symbolic peril to be suppressed.

Related to views of order and wholeness is the symbol of *health*. Prosperous people might not always be healthy, but they have the means to seek the care or intervention by which health may eventually be restored. Moreover, basic foundations for good health like adequate nutrition and shelter are already a part of their ordinary existence. By contrast, we were struck by how frequently the pastors we interviewed used the language of health (or its loss) as a metaphor for the more general struggles among their lower-class parishioners.

Interestingly, however, the language itself made reference not to disease but to addiction. A pastor from central California spoke of this in terms we heard nationwide.

> Among our poor people here, addiction is a very big problem, not only of substances but also to violence and other kinds of things. So to bring healing and sanity and tranquility to their lives has a lot to do with putting away addictions and helping people struggle on a day-to-day basis to get past their addictions. It means taking steps toward liberation, where the people actually get free and can be themselves.

Obviously, addiction can and does afflict all classes. What this remark and others like it conveys, however, is that threats to health among lower classes were persistently spoken of as addictive challenges. In various facets of physical or emotional well-being, life could be overtaken in a way that was not simply disabling or enslaving but even self-depleting. As a result, restoration to health (again, not just physical but also emotional and social) required a kind of intervention or conversion never mentioned in reference to upper classes. For lower classes, healthy living is less a path on level ground than a stroll near the edge of a cliff.

Such threats to existence highlight a third symbol: *security*. When social supports are abundant, daily life is taken for granted and never comes into serious question. When assaults to order and health take their toll, however, the outlook is far less confident and assured. Pastors in mixed class settings spoke of the basic level of fear that could separate lower classes from all others. While any group might easily become afraid, of course, the kind of fears in lower-class groups derived from experiences of actual harm rather than perceived or projected threats.

As a result, several preachers we interviewed pointed out a distinctive kind of conservative behavior that such fear evoked in their poorer parishioners. Instead of being risk-takers with little to lose or revolutionaries looking for radical changes, these people could be surprisingly traditionalistic. One pastor clarified how this was part of a larger set of life strategies.

> These people are conservative by nature. They've had to be conservative folk in order to survive and get along in the world. I think part of it has to do with the fact that they have, within their families, been subjected to outside forces that have challenged them and caused them to have to struggle to come through times of economic distress. But they are not ideological conservatives. I think that there's a toleration of different lifestyles, of people having problems. I've been surprised at how loving and compassionate and tolerant these folks are of people who are struggling. They are not judgmental people. They don't have their minds made up about things.

It is important to recognize that, given the assaults to life mentioned already, such conservative behavior among lower classes is an entirely sensible response. If life is fragile and insecure, then reducing risks and minimizing changes are fitting strategies for survival. In light of all this, other pastors we interviewed stressed the importance of avoiding whatever might provoke instability or personal shame in lives that were already tenuous.

When people are oriented by the symbols of order, health, and security, it is no surprise that they are also more able to look ahead with a certain measure of *hope*. For those with strong economic, social, and educational resources, for example, the future is a vista shining with potential. Lacking these capacities, however, persons in a lower class may well envision the path ahead only in terms of the dim course their lives have already taken. If tomorrow means simply more of the same, there may obviously be little reason for encouragement.

Those we interviewed spoke of poorer persons in their congregations whose enduring limitations and nagging failures left them mired in despair. Just as we saw with health, so also hope was not some reality on which one could ordinarily depend. As a symbol, hope represented something always subject to loss, something requiring dramatic action in order to be restored. Referring to this challenge, one preacher told of the slim resources within the blue-collar households of his congregation. Because of this long-standing situation, these persons had been trained to have a fear of failure that also robbed them of any clear vision. His ongoing goal was simply to name the signs of hope that were evident in their lives. Another pastor cautioned, however, how difficult it is to do this credibly. The vulnerable of society have been so frequently betrayed by false dreams that they are deeply cynical. The church first must clearly say, "Life is more than economics," he argued, and then be equally clear about a faithfulness that transcends cheap and cheery optimism.

Preaching Strategies

Despite the erosion of public esteem that some say ministry has suffered, pastors continue to operate in a sphere of social privilege. Due to professional identity and education (and sometimes income), they typically benefit in the overall scheme of class. Even when one's own personal background has been of a lower class, the simple fact of holding pastoral office socially relocates an individual and reinforces new ways of thinking and acting. As a result, preachers often easily lose touch with how to speak beyond this professionally achieved social location. Starting with themselves, our informants realized the challenge of learning how to operate outside the class role they had adopted simply through being a pastor.

What preachers need to learn, however, is not some bag of tricks for becoming appealingly relevant to other classes. Instead, our informants suggested strategies rooted in the deepest realities of being human, sometimes called "material universals." It is no small thing, for example, that despite all our differences, class and otherwise, everyone hungers and can be wounded and cannot live alone. These basic, common realities may be felt most acutely by the poor to whom these remain gaping needs, but they are known by us all. No wonder, then, that these same universals are at the heart of such potent salvific metaphors as feeding, healing, and community.

While this might not seem very important for preaching, it is in fact when we ignore these core, material realities that we provoke both suffering in deed and irrelevance in word. When pastors pay attention to this basic level of existence, however, their preaching matters for all classes because it addresses the heart of human experience. For these reasons, our respondents recommended the tools of embodied reference, familiar knowledge, and liberative vision as strategies for cross-cultural preachers who want to take seriously the frame of class.

Embodied Reference

Earlier in this chapter, we reported that our interviewees remarked about different thought processes that tended to characterize different classes. Those remarks included the observation that people in economically difficult circumstances more regularly appealed to concrete situations, personal experiences, and effective practices as a preferred warrant for reasoning. When it came to suggesting strategies for preaching, then, these same interviewees overwhelmingly urged a kind of language that embodied daily life and was embedded in ordinary experience, rather than resorting to concepts and abstractions. We discerned that these preachers meant at least three related things by this suggestion.

First, embodied reference is *concretely derived*. A pastor serving in a rapidly changing neighborhood with wide class disparities between old-timers and newcomers felt that the worst thing he could do is to remain silent about the specific community realities facing his congregation. "We like to personalize our sins. But in the sermon, I'll bring up social concerns. Many times, I'll bring in things that have taken place in the neighborhood, like even a recent killing or a shooting, for example, or the way certain neighborhood pockets around the church are fighting back to have slumlords get their property back in shape. So I talk a lot about community and what that means." Since all of his listeners already knew of what was happening in the neighborhood, this pastor refused to let those issues become privatized, spiritualized, suppressed, or abstracted. The more he spoke of the concrete events in the surrounding area, the more he touched on concerns that were shared across class lines.

While this advice about concreteness may seem rather obvious, the simple fact that so many interviewees recommended it suggests that, in their experience, few other preachers actually put this insight into practice. Moreover, respondents did not advocate a steady diet of references to daily life but instead a more subtle and differentiated approach. One pastor in a self-described working-class congregation began her remarks on the subject as did many others with whom we spoke. "The gospel here needs to be preached in such a way that it does not deal with abstractions, but deals concretely with real life problems. The jargon for it here is, 'Where the rubber meets the road.' Doctrine and principle, that kind of a sermon, will not speak here."

Later in the same interview, however, this pastor modified her advice in an intriguing way.

> While the working-class values and lifestyle here is more or less what I grew up in, I'd say my family today is probably the first generation to be more white collar than not. So in a sense, I know [working-class life] very well, but it's not where I live now. And one of the things that is a turnoff is if I try to speak with too much authority about the lives of parishioners. It's weird, because it needs to be concrete but it doesn't work well if it's too direct, if it really just is right on where they live. There needs to be a little bit of distance. The healing and wound imagery is helpful. You don't want to poke at the wound too directly. You want to touch it and say, "I see this wound," but you need to be gentle about it.

Being concrete does not call for relentless recitation of every difficult detail of life. Instead, this pastor urged a kind of gentle naming that was just as specific and honest while avoiding the risks of harming her congregants or presenting herself as an expert.

Others also mentioned that concretely derived preaching may call for indirectness. One respondent discussed a Mother's Day sermon in a lower-class community that had many dysfunctional families. The holiday itself provoked conflicting reactions among the women present who knew they had often failed as mothers but still longed for something better. This pastor therefore spoke in concrete yet indirect terms.

> I left Mother's Day for a little bit and talked about small feet. I told a story about me always falling as a child because my feet were too small. I kept hurting my knees all the time when I was little, and my mother took care of that. I was so sad because I usually couldn't run, and she would tend to this. And then I talked about the different roads in life that we go on, how many times we fall down, who tends to us, and why the mother is not there. And a lot of these mothers [in the congregation] have deserted their kids and that's their road, and it's been so hard for them. Then I made a concrete connection with the feet of Christ. I had comments days after the sermon where they would use feet and road, the smallness of their feet and my feet, connected with the feet of Jesus on that road.

Note that this pastor drew upon an accessible experience while bypassing direct references to family dysfunction, in order to permit hearers to connect for themselves with these more difficult concrete realities.

A second feature that we discerned from our interviews is that embodied reference is *emotionally engaged*. One urban pastor described what he thought his economically diverse members looked for in sermons. "They would expect the preacher to speak in a style that engages them emotionally, to have passion, and certainly not read a manuscript in a dispassionate intellectualized style. I think they would expect a sermon that would have some humor in it, and also that would not be afraid to touch some of the raw emotions that people feel in life."

The implicit suggestion here is not emotionalism for its own sake but identifying with the deep feelings already present in specific and significant experiences. When these feelings are named in preaching, then those who bear them are addressed at a level of existence far deeper than the merely intellectual. The playing field now becomes a common ground of affective responses and moods that all classes equally inhabit.

Our respondents identified two important ways emotional engagement could be signaled, both of which have potential as preaching strategies. One was through music and hymns that could directly express underlying emotions. Obviously, musical tastes are loaded with class values and present challenges familiar to any pastor. One interviewee contrasted his present and former congregations along such lines.

> I think that from a musical point of view, and this does relate to socioeconomic context, there is a different interest and resonance. They resonate here with different things musically than where I've been previously. People there were open to different music, too, but were more likely to be going in the direction of fairly classical presentations of music. Here, things are *really* different. People are really attracted to gospel-flavored kind of stuff—Fanny Crosby and late-nineteenth-century or early-twentieth-century gospel hymns that are very emotive. We have bluegrass musicians in this church, banjos and guitars, and they are doing a real gospel-oriented tradition. The choir sometimes sings with a taped accompaniment, which would have just horrified people in my previous congregation.

Familiar as this contrast may be, these remarks also underscore that the emotional engagement of music be taken seriously across all class situations. Interviewees often spoke of stretching into styles of music they found unfamiliar or unattractive in order to hear the feelings and moods of church members. This effort was eventually rewarded, however, by the ability to use hymn lyrics in preaching, for example, or develop a powerful musical conclusion to a sermon.

The larger point is to claim the vast potential in music to activate memories and experiences among diverse classes of hearers.

Another way emotional engagement can be signaled is through drama. Preaching embodies emotions more effectively for many groups, we were told, by enacting the message being proclaimed. One pastor remarked, "If I assume the role or voice of a biblical character and work that a little bit, I think they fall into it, enjoy it, draw power from it." More than being an entertaining device, this dramatic strategy aims at engaging hearers more fully with a truly "embodied" preaching event. Another pastor wrote scripted dialogues for use with biblical texts on emotionally explosive topics like divorce or adultery. Sermons unfolded like an ordinary conversation between two persons. Alternative views were concretely named and tested in a way that hearers could overhear without feeling directly challenged. Attention was thus focused on the content of the dialogue itself rather than a solitary preacher whose words might be misconstrued as confrontational or authoritarian.

A third aspect of embodied reference is that it is *personally exhibited*. In the end, the preacher is the one through whom any sermon becomes specific and concrete, and this implies several preaching strategies about delivery. One of these is quite consistent with what we learned through the frame of ethnicity in chapter 2: greater attention to orality. From a scholarly perspective, Walter Ong's discussion of primary oral societies (see Suggested Readings) remains foundational for understanding this matter. From a pastoral perspective, our interviewees urged several strategies for making the preacher more directly present to the hearers in order that the sermon itself might become a more embodied event.

The most typical suggestion we heard was to eliminate the use of a complete manuscript while preaching. This advice was not the result of lazy sermon preparation but rather a desire to link sermon presentation with how people ordinarily communicate in the congregation. One pastor simply remarked, "It's not that the folks here can't read. They certainly can, but [this church] is part of a community that just functions more out of an oral tradition." Abandoning the manuscript was not easy, however, as another of our respondents remarked:

> I'm still writing out my sermon, but I've been delivering it without a manuscript. I find that it's scary for me to do that, because I did it the other way, with a complete manuscript, for so long. But I find that what I'm losing in precision and perhaps eloquence by being willing to leave the manuscript behind is being more than compensated by what I'm sensing I'm gaining in connectedness with the congregation. Perhaps it goes along with being more cautious about the intricacies of a scholarly debate or Greek word studies or whatever else I might have been inclined to write in a manuscript in other contexts.

The trade-off mentioned above is not superficial. To change something as apparently small as sermon notation may also mean moving away from the preferred warrants for reasoning of one class (precision and eloquence) and toward those of another class (personal connection).

Connected with the question of manuscript use, orality was also enhanced when the preacher changed the delivery location. This usually meant leaving the pulpit and speaking from the midst of the assembly. Such relocation not only created closer proximity with hearers but also allowed the entire physical frame of the preacher to convey the message. "Instead of standing in one place with only your shoulders and head showing," said one pastor, "when I come out from behind the pulpit, I'm able to utilize my hands more and be freer from looking down, and there's more of an emotional connection." The preacher's whole body, when used with skill, offers more levels for communicating with the assembly than words alone.

As for other matters of delivery that the preacher might personally exhibit in embodying the sermon, we heard far less consensus. Length of sermon was one of these areas, with respondents making compelling yet opposite arguments for why one class group preferred longer or shorter sermons than another. The role of extended silence or slower pace of delivery had a similarly contradictory set of responses. Even with this lack of agreement, however, these preachers still knew exactly how specific class conditions in their respective settings affected decisions about these delivery questions, which is itself an important strategy for any cross-cultural preacher.

There was substantially more agreement, however, in one last area. Interviewees saw an important opportunity to reach across class lines by personally exhibiting appropriate humor. In part, this relates to what was said about orality, since humor operates to signal an informal, affective connection typical of social interaction in orally oriented groups. At a more substantive level, however, humor provides a valuable strategy for looking at difficult or unpleasant subjects in a less threatening way. It holds up a mirror in which people can see their own plight reflected first through the absurdity of an outside situation. It works in a way quite similar to what we heard earlier about being both concrete and indirect, providing a moment of distance that leads to a subsequent connection.

None of these strategies for personally exhibiting a more embodied sermon was offered as an absolute. Most of our interviewees in fact viewed multiple and flexible strategies in mixed class congregations to be the most effective approach, as one pastor from a West Coast city described at length. "About half my sermons I preach from the pulpit with a printed manuscript, which I don't read but I basically follow. The other half I preach out of the pulpit with no notes, standing right before the people. Since the pulpit is high up, these others still have to be delivered from the chancel and not the sanctuary floor, but still much closer to them so that occasionally I could even walk down the steps and touch someone."

Building on this description of styles, this pastor went on to discuss the range of impact these styles evoked.

> I have noticed that clearly the different styles give rise to different levels of authority assigned to the sermon. In general, those with a higher socioeconomic level, with higher education, or those who have a long tradition in the church seem to give more authority to the sermon when it is delivered from the pulpit with the manuscript. In general, those who have a lower socioeconomic level, those who have less education, or those who are newer in the church and perhaps newer in the Christian faith tend to give more authority to a sermon delivered out of the pulpit. They tell me it seems like I'm much more open, honest, genuine, more intimate in style. And of course, I tend in fact to preach a more intimate type of sermon, more narrative perhaps, or more humor, or more personal stories, and it's more dramatic. It has an air of theater about it. I can use a pause or use my body much differently when I'm not confined to a pulpit. But in both cases, whether I'm in the pulpit or in the chancel, whether it's for folks who are higher socioeconomic level or lower, I think all of them tend to give a good deal of authority to the sermon, more than I would usually expect.

We noted earlier that contrasting views of authority result from different class experiences. This pastor's comment reminds us that matters of delivery can trigger these views of authority within any one class, and not always in good ways. Fortunately for our purposes, however, when a sermon is concretely derived, emotionally engaged, and personally exhibited, people from many classes are more likely to hear and accept its claim within their respective circumstances.

Familiar Knowledge

One ancient rule in classical rhetoric is to develop familiar themes ("agreement," as it was called) before moving to newer ideas and proposals. This rule was no abstract ideal but simply expressed a commonsense observation about how most people are persuaded. We heard a similar observation from many of our informants. They reported that effective preaching in mixed class settings built upon what was already familiar (a matter of substance) and sought to make familiar whatever was being presented (a matter of design).

When our interviewees spoke of building upon what was already familiar, they did not mean merely repeating what people already knew. Instead, we understood them to be referring to something we have come to call *binding language*. We have already seen that sermons reach across class lines when their references are concretely derived. These concrete references have the ability to bind people together regardless of class situation because everyone has shared in the community life that sponsored them. Symbols and practices, rhythms and patterns, stories of strength or crisis all produce a dense fabric of images and concepts of which everyone is aware. These are like a common code that insiders have learned and outsiders need to learn if they wish to participate. Effective cross-cultural preachers use such codes to bind all of their hearers into the preaching event, and in a way that avoids class segregation.

This sort of language is binding in another way, however. In many cases, our interviewees noted that such language also expresses the limitations of a particular congregation. One pastor learned over time that the values, relationships, and even foods that served as common codes in her congregation had attained that status because of the limited economic and social conditions of the members. These codes were binding in the sense that they expressed local constraints. To be sure, such language remained an important expression of familiar knowledge in the congregation upon which she could draw. At the same time, however, it also marked a boundary that could not be crossed without alienating many of the members. In a similar setting of economic hardship, another pastor noted that he rarely referred to the many places he has lived or traveled, since such opportunities were simply not present for most of his lower-class parishioners. Knowing the language that binds a community together also means realizing the constraints such language imposes and living within these when preaching.

Another set of suggestions by preachers in mixed class settings focused not on common codes upon which one might build but on the common direction all hearers might follow. Instead of grounding the sermon in something already familiar, this instead involved making the sermon increasingly familiar as it progressed. These strategies we have labeled *directive design*. They are devices for arranging the sermon that give guidance like a handrail, both reassuring hearers that they are on the right path and reinforcing the message being heard.

Chief among these strategies recommended in interviews was that of repetition, an approach also mentioned in relation to the frames of ethnicity and displacement. One pastor contrasted his writing style (making a point only once and with correct grammar) to his preaching style, where he "repeats things over and over again" with little attention to proper rules. This is not sloppy thinking but instead being sensitive to matters of orality, permitting hearers multiple chances to grasp what is being said. Beyond this, repetition provides a means for addressing the same topic in language that appeals to different classes. With members ranging from "mid-level management types to folks on disability and food stamps," another pastor spoke of a recent sermon where repetition was used in this way.

What I did was begin with a quote about codependency. It was from a technical, psychological textbook, and the quote was one which probably would have been appreciated by those who have some understanding of psychological processes and therapy, the kind of academic approach to these things. Then, I spoke about the very same thing in very simple terms about my own longing for spring and my own sense of winter as wading through mud. As I used it, this lawyer sitting right there was probably not grooving on this very much, but I could tell from the responses of so many others that they were very much in tune with the personal illustration in which I used very simple language, evocative language, emotional language. I even used my body and moved in a way that was probably too provocative for the more academically oriented, intellectual, higher socioeconomic folks sitting there. And yet I had earlier used that quote from a text recognizing that they would probably appreciate that kind of expression.

In this case, repetition served primarily to guide and reassure all hearers and secondarily (but not insignificantly) to appeal to different class groups.

Another strategy of directive design is related to the use of aesthetic devices. We have already mentioned how music, for example, can make preaching more emotionally engaged with one or more classes of hearers. At this point, however, we are focusing on the way aesthetic devices like music, visual arts, and storytelling can make the message of the sermon more familiar to hearers. One preacher told us that her goal in referring to such devices was "to create connections halfway" between the unfolding sermon (unfamiliar element) and an aesthetic form already found in daily life (familiar element).

The use of narratives was a specific kind of aesthetic device mentioned frequently, but it is important to hear the full range of what our interviewees intended. At a basic level, of course, the use of familiar local stories is a way of linking the emerging sermon to something concretely derived from daily experience. At a richer level, however, the very flow of any narrative offers a guide and reassurance to hearers even if they have never heard that specific story before. This is because effective narratives create expectations that people want to have satisfied. A mystery, for example, evokes an expectation that some puzzle will finally be solved, even though that resolution may be long in coming. This anticipatory energy draws people into the unfolding story itself and anything connected to it. Therefore, the purpose of this strategy in effective cross-cultural preaching is not so much to select familiar stories as to use a narrative design that maintains involvement through a process of anticipation. This directive capacity of any narrative is what appeals across class lines.

One final directive device to consider is the pattern of the biblical text to which the sermon is related. Referring to preaching without a manuscript, one pastor also noted that his sermons now followed the shape of the scripture reading. "I'm relying more on a series of established movements within the text," he said, "and trying to be as familiar as I can with what I want to accomplish in each movement as I go through the sermon." In other words, the form of the biblical text, usually read aloud just before the sermon and perhaps quite familiar to the hearers, was guiding the shape of the sermon itself. It therefore served to support and reinforce the direction the sermon would eventually take.

Of course, there are also many ways that preachers can inadvertently subvert these directive devices. Repeatedly we heard a warning to stay simple in mixed class settings—not simplistic or banal, but focused on a core message reinforced in multiple ways. One experienced preacher confessed her own struggles with "trying to say too much and either going in too many directions or having a single direction that's too complex." Another had learned to use self-monitoring devices in preparing and presenting sermons, looking for "short words, short sentences, strong motivations, and asking folks, 'Did you understand what I said?'" A third interviewee was guided by a fundamental rule in trying to keep his hearers on track: "The key to me being able to communicate with the people in this congregation is to speak the language they speak. That isn't often fancy words. It was, I think, really to learn to speak the lingo of the people, their dialect." In summary, then, our informants had learned to be intentional both in using directive devices and in avoiding whatever might derail.

Liberative Vision

Up to this point, we have reported from our interviews various preaching strategies that enhance a kind of stability. Strategies of embodied reference, for instance, accentuate extant circumstances and experiences. In a similar way, strategies of familiar knowledge develop from what is already known and available. In looking beyond these methods that enhance stability, our informants also alerted us to preaching strategies that emphasize change. In particular, they highlighted the use of scripture in mixed class settings that could create a liberative vision.

Appealing to scripture for such a vision is consistent with something mentioned earlier in this chapter. An important characteristic across all class lines, we noted, was the serious place given to scriptural authority. The *manner* in which the Bible is authoritative may differ widely from one class to another, but the *fact* of its authority remains uncontested. No wonder, then, that so many of our interviewees used scripture as a common point of departure in mixed class congregations in order to direct all their hearers toward a broader vista of God's healing and hope.

At the same time, however, there was little agreement among these preachers about which portions of the canon were better suited to portray this liberative vision. Some preferred basic and familiar narratives from the synoptic gospels and the Old Testament, complaining that Johannine texts were too abstract and epistolary materials too dense. Others, by contrast, relied on epistles precisely because they referred to concrete struggles and divisions analogous to those in their own congregations. While some respondents turned to prophetic texts that directly confronted economic and social injustice, others flatly avoided these due to the risk of alienating certain hearers.

Regardless of these differences, however, the use of any biblical text was clearly affected by what we earlier referred to as the symbolic burdens of class. We especially learned that the liberative vision of scripture is filtered through class-specific views of security and hope. Interviewees mentioned times when a text about divine justice or social reversal simply could not be heard by certain congregants because it threatened traditional understandings or provoked already shaky situations. Even in offering a liberative vision through preaching, we heard of the need to move from a basic reassurance toward a call for repentance and renewal.

For these reasons, many of those we interviewed regularly returned in their preaching to biblical visions of *nurture*. One pastor who was very committed to a prophetic kind of preaching surprisingly remarked that it simply would not work in her lower-class congregation to preach a steady diet of social issues. "The pastoral care needs are pretty high," she said, "with a great need for nurture, and so a lot of shepherd imagery has been very powerful to use with them." Comparable texts about healing, feeding, reconnecting, and guiding contributed to this vision of nurture, appealing broadly to many classes in no small measure because they built upon the material universals we mentioned before. Indeed, such nurture is itself profoundly liberative because it speaks to the actual needs and trials people already are facing. As one pastor put it, "God's care for the poor must surely mean God cares for these people," which in turn means nothing less than freedom.

Building on this language of nurture was a call for *justice* in cross-cultural preaching. This often meant using narratives in which hearers from different classes could identify with different characters. However, since class identity already internalizes social separations, we were cautioned that this strategy must name injustice without inflaming division. All hearers should see themselves standing under the text's accusation and promise, as one pastor explained:

> On these texts that have to do with wealth, I'm well aware that when I speak of those who have wealth and need to be generous, many of those hearing will not think of themselves in that category and so may not feel that the text speaks to them. But comparatively speaking on global terms, there's not a person in this church who is not wealthy in some way. So I'll say that the principle of the text may sound like it's aimed only at those who have great riches, but it certainly applies to every one of us.

Contrasts between rich and poor were not the only biblical resource for evoking a vision of justice. Some preachers said it was just as useful to build a connection between their own hearers and the experiences or attitudes of textual characters:

> Let's take the Prodigal Son. I might be asking some of our people to hear that parable through the older son, the one who stayed behind, the one who was steady, the one who did what he was supposed to do, and was part of the successful household. But there would also be a number of people here who would be more likely to perhaps identify with the prodigal: coming home. Or in the case of the Rich Man and Lazarus, it's a challenging word to think about how they might share the attitudes of the rich man, because people in this congregation are not beggars at the door but neither are they those who are represented by the man who lived behind the gates and never saw poor Lazarus.

Whatever the case, this approach lets hearers adopt roles that fit them while also leading them into a liberative vision drawn from scripture. Like the use of indirectness and even humor, it is a preaching strategy by which different classes can hear both challenge and promise without being reduced to or condemned for their class identity.

4. The Frame of Displacement

Vanessa's new office was still cluttered, and most of her books remained in boxes. The stress of moving, however, was offset by the excitement and anticipation of beginning ministry in a new place. Having served a dozen years in her first call in an open-country rural setting, she was now the pastor of a downtown church in one of the largest cities in the state. Eager volunteers and excellent facilities, resources sorely lacking in her previous setting, were lavishly abundant now. The tripling of her salary practically overnight did not escape her notice, either. Although comfortable with rural life from both her upbringing and her parish service, Vanessa privately realized that she was now in the big leagues. Sitting in the office of her own tall-steeple church in the heart of the city, she was ready for it to be great.

No sooner had she settled in than she began visiting, teaching, and leading worship—the same things she had done in her previous churches. Vanessa was surprised to discover, however, that although she was the same person performing basically the same tasks, it all felt somehow different and even a little awkward. Perhaps it was just a matter of adjusting to a new place and new people. *Give yourself some time,* she thought.

In time, the moving boxes disappeared but the unsettled feelings did not. After six months, when parishioners asked how she was doing, Vanessa responded with the customary "Fine." It wasn't really the truth, and she puzzled over why she still felt the same anxiety she had known when she first arrived. Her eyes could see all she had, but her heart knew something else was missing. Time passed, and her concerns grew. She remained in bed each morning longer than she ever had in the country, not at all eager to arise and begin the day. There was nothing wrong with her new congregation or the people in it. The problem must be with her, she thought, and so self-blame compounded her lack of energy. She even began to wonder whether she should continue being a pastor.

Finally, eleven months into her new pastorate Vanessa made a hospital call that gave her a startling new perspective. She visited a woman named Maria who had immigrated from Mexico to the United States five years earlier. Maria was a widow now living with her son and his family. When Vanessa entered Maria's room, *The Wizard of Oz* was playing on the television, and Maria was crying. Vanessa recalled what happened next:

> I asked Maria if she was all right. She told me that she knew this movie. She had seen it before, and it made her very happy. She loved it that Dorothy could make a wish, click her heels together, and suddenly be back home in Kansas. But then, she also said that the movie made her feel very sad and empty. She was thankful to have a nice home with her son and daughter-in-law and grandchildren, but she wanted to return to her real home. She wanted to go home, back to Mexico. She knew that wishing and heel-clicking would not make it happen. Many things in her life were good now, but she wanted to go home. As Maria said this, it just hit me. Standing in a hospital room with Munchkins singing in the background, I realized Maria was describing my sadness and emptiness as well.

Some readers may not see Vanessa's new realization as being especially significant. After all, isn't simple homesickness just a problem for children, something that happens during the first day or two of summer camp? Others may find it surprising that Vanessa was so unaware of what caused her own feelings. We have learned through our research, however, that the very tendency to dismiss and thus ignore this issue has not only profound pastoral consequences but also significant cross-cultural implications that bear upon preaching.

We therefore introduce *displacement* as a cultural frame by which we mean any movement or shift from a customary setting. The customary settings in our lives are those spaces where we usually experience familiarity, predictability, and control—wherever we feel safe. Psychologists note that when people are displaced in this sense, they can experience culture shock: an emotional reaction that follows from not being able to understand and predict one's environment. When people move to a new place, for example, their lack of familiarity with such things as time use, ritual, and even simple etiquette can lead to a perceived loss of control regarding their new environment and the people with whom they must now interact.

As Vanessa's story indicates, displacement can first produce an overwhelming sense of *isolation*. Frequently this isolation drives the sufferer inward. It is difficult to share feelings with others because, to all external appearances, things seem to be fine, perhaps even exceptional. Compounding this isolation is a sense of *ambivalence* about one's own feelings. Displaced persons are caught in a dilemma. On the one hand, they know they have good reason to be pleased about a new situation. On the other hand, though, they are plagued by a loss that cannot be restored. Since this ambivalence grows over time, displacement can become an *enduring* problem that never seems to go away. Most of us expect some feelings of loss in the immediate wake of a move. We tend to underestimate, however, that this can still afflict well-adjusted adults years later, shaping their worldview and sense of contentment.

This layered impact of displacement seems to be why Maria was such a catalyst for Vanessa's realization. Only through the mirror of another person's experience could Vanessa name her own displacement. Our encounter with Vanessa led us to wonder how many other members of congregations might be similarly affected because of the rapid cultural changes around us. Given this, what would it then mean for preachers to speak comfort and hope to those who culturally never feel fully at home? Our task in this chapter is to acknowledge displacement as a legitimate and pervasive cultural frame that can significantly affect the way hearers experience sermons. Again, we will structure our interview findings around *group characteristics* and *preaching strategies*. In order to lay the groundwork for that discussion, however, we will first consider the *causes* of displacement. While Vanessa's story presented an instance of displacement related to locale, it is important also to examine displacement in terms of time and belonging. We will then discuss the *effects* of displacement, which will suggest certain goals for dealing with this complex challenge and the role that preaching might come to play.

Cause and Effect

The frame of displacement may not be nearly as familiar a way of considering culture as those of ethnicity, class, or beliefs. Even so, as we have already noted, displacement has a profound impact on many people. Recall for a moment our earlier definition of culture. We introduced culture as "the ways we mark off who we are and give shape to the spaces we inhabit." We also spoke of it as "a human construct that includes both our patterns of meaning and our strategies for action." It is precisely these things that are undercut by displacement. Displacement separates us from the patterns that have been central to us, the strategies that have helped us mark off who we are. Unlike ethnicity, class, and beliefs, the cultural frame of displacement does not provide a particular kind of marking off and shaping. On the contrary, displacement threatens the very core of what culture at its best seeks to provide. Displacement is actually an "anti-culture" cultural frame that undermines the very benefits culture can give: ways toward identity, belonging, and action.

We include displacement as one of the cultural frames in this research because its impact on people and how they hear sermons can be significant. Displacement robs a person of the necessary interpretive resources that culture typically provides. Its impact is therefore far more extensive than merely affecting the private emotional lives of scattered individuals. Displacement, understood as a cultural frame, is disruptive at the level of one's worldview. As such, it is something for preachers to take quite seriously.

Being separated from that which establishes familiarity, predictability, and control can cause feelings ranging from mild discomfort to significant fear of perceived danger. The latter is perhaps most poignantly seen in settings where the importance of place is expressed ritually. For example, in much of Southeast Asia there is a widespread practice of burying the placenta nearby when a baby is born. Traditional Cambodian healers say that the location of the burial is critical. They explain that the placenta is the "globe of the origin of the soul" of the child. If the placenta is buried and kept safe, the child will also remain safe, provided she or he does not stray too far. This practice vividly expresses the local belief that people are safe when they remain at home but enter a state of danger when they move away.

This ritual, although not widely practiced outside Southeast Asia, can serve as a metaphor for the danger that many people experience in displacement tied to *locale*, such as a move away from the customary setting of the home. For large numbers of people, such a move is forced upon them. The United Nations reports that one out of every 130 people on earth has been forced into flight. Beyond the twenty-three million who are international refugees, there are another thirty million internally displaced persons. Voluntary and forced migration has been and continues to be one of the most persistent themes of human history.

While it is obvious that the cultural frame of displacement applies most clearly to those who have immigrated to the United States from other countries, those born in America are not immune. Displacement is a cultural issue of some considerable magnitude for native-born Americans as well. William Leach (see Suggested Readings) notes how an entire subculture of rootless people has grown up in the United States. He speaks of the spread of "a landscape of the temporary" that is populated by both skilled and unskilled persons who are willing or compelled to go anywhere to find work. Americans no longer tend to live and die in the same place. This is true for all economic levels of our society. Middle-class professionals have been described as the new migrant workers, especially during the early years of their careers.

The typical perception is that most Americans have adapted to the geographical mobility of contemporary life with relative ease and little anxiety. Unfortunately, this perception does not coincide with lived experience. Even moves of relatively short distances can often generate a great deal of stress. Researchers report that two factors, the absence of people with whom someone was close and the duration of time since a move, play a much greater role in the degree of anxiety experienced than the distance an individual has actually moved. Thus, even people moving from "just the next county" can still experience the powerfully negative effects of displacement. One woman with whom we spoke who had moved only a short distance said, "I felt as if my heart was taken out of me."

Up to this point we have limited our treatment of displacement to matters of locale. However, *time* can also be a factor in causing displacement. Nostalgia is a sentimental longing for bygone days. The expression originates from the Greek *nostos* ("to return home") + *algos* ("pain"). Nostalgia is therefore the temporal analogue to the kind of "homesickness" we have described above. People may have an intense, almost unbearable longing for home even though they may still be living in the house in which they were born. Their longing is for a different time, and their pain may be connected with and based on the joy they felt when they were younger. Significant for our purposes here, experiences of God may also be embedded in and constrained by those earlier days, so that feelings of nostalgia can for some people also include a loss of God.

This nostalgic sense of displacement can be present in any geographical context. It may, for example, be a serious issue even in rural settings where change seems slow and there appears to be little need for intentional, cross-cultural preaching. Rural residents sometimes comment on how life dramatically changed when others moved into their community. Persons who have spent their entire lives engaged in agriculture may feel severe displacement when newcomers contribute to an ethos that no longer feels rural in the ways it always had before. Traditional, time-honored ideals of community life come under assault through new neighbors like industrial poultry operations, upwardly mobile suburbanites, and methamphetamine labs. In such cases, lifelong community members report feeling like they now live in a foreign country, longing for the good old days.

Finally, displacement is not limited only to changes in locale or time. A change in the sense of *belonging* between individuals and the groups significant to them, let alone the larger society in which they are grounded, can also cause displacement. When people lose a sense of attachment to what anchors them socially, they can experience a kind of displacement that is best described as "alienation."

In earlier times, to alienate something meant to transfer its ownership. Thus when Karl Marx used the term, he referred to commodities or labor that had been sold for money as having been alienated. In similar ways, people still speak of "alienation of affection" when they feel that someone's love has been stolen. Persons not in full possession of themselves or their faculties were once treated by specialists called "alienists," a term commonly used in Great Britain to refer to those we now generally recognize as psychiatrists.

Today, alienation is commonly used to refer to feeling like a stranger in relation to persons or actions. One no longer holds or commands a familiar, predictable, and controlled role in the relationship. A quarrel is said to alienate friends from one another. The word is used in a wider sense when people speak of being alienated from their work or even from their bodies or themselves. When people say they are alienated, they sometimes speak of a sense of depersonalization and aimlessness, an isolation that permeates life like a damp fog. For these reasons, alienation serves as a powerful metaphor for the relational dimension and impact of displacement. The displaced are aliens, estranged from persons they have known all their lives. They are outsiders in their own families. Even in speaking, they are forced to use a language through which they cannot make themselves understood.

There are, of course, many potential triggers for this displacement from belonging. Of particular significance for our purposes is the trigger of work, not least of all because of its overlaps with the affects of the cultural frame of class. For example, people can become cut off from the work world through layoff or retirement and thus be alienated from a sphere of life that provides significant, reliable relationships. Thus, we learned that alienation for blue-collar males typically is expressed in connection with work because a core sense of belonging is found there, even for those who detest their jobs.

Whether the cause of displacement is tied to changes in locale, time, or belonging, the speed by which such changes are experienced can range on a continuum from the instantaneous to the exceptionally slow. Homesickness can occur overnight through immigration, or it may stretch across many years, as when a neighborhood in a once stable community is gradually altered by the advent of new neighbors. Nostalgia can be felt immediately when a loved one dies, or grow by almost imperceptible gradations through the process of aging or the bit-by-bit onset of disability. Alienation may assert itself with almost revolutionary force in the wake of a lost job, or take a more subtle and evolutionary course when loved ones drift ever so slowly apart.

Having considered three causes of displacement (change in locale, time, and belonging), we now turn to its effects. Readers of this book will likely be familiar with some of the effects of displacement through firsthand experience, effects reminiscent of those stages we encounter with any form of loss. Due to the loss of key people, settings, objects, capacities, experiences, patterns, and countless other core realities of daily life, displacement can make itself felt in at least four important areas: identity, anomie, rejection, and grief.

Since, as noted earlier, displacement functions as an anti-culture cultural frame, it deprives people of an ordinary source of *identity* development and confirmation and thus produces a dilemma concerning the sense of self. International immigrants, in particular, frequently struggle with confusion about their proper role and its expectations in a new place. This can be compounded by feelings of deprivation concerning the professional abilities and related status left behind in one's homeland and not honored in a new place of residence. In a similar way, when people face a dramatically new worldview or lose touch with meaningful personal contacts, the tools for guiding and testing human identity are at least partly undercut.

Another effect of displacement can be *anomie:* feelings of powerlessness, meaninglessness, normlessness, and social isolation. Displaced persons have lost the social networks that provided their emotional support system. This is particularly true when a person is not fluent in the dominant language of the new setting, and can remain an issue even in regard to local or regional dialects. The limitation of language reinforces a sense of emotional and social isolation. Such isolation includes not only the loss of comfort and security that comes from hearing one's own spoken language. It also extends to the loss of the accompanying nonverbal communication, where misunderstandings often have a longer-lasting effect than verbal ones.

Anomie for the displaced can be further aggravated by feelings of *rejection* from those already residing in the new and unfamiliar setting. This is obviously true when hostility toward immigrants or social changes erupts. Even when these neighbors try to greet and include the new arrivals, however, displaced persons may find it difficult to experience that welcome fully. The sense of welcome may be diminished by an internal clash between the displaced person's own values and those of the new place. Even though this subtle kind of rejection emerges from within the displaced person rather than being imposed by the social setting, it nonetheless retains a vivid impact upon those adjusting to new situations.

Each of the effects considered so far is accompanied by a sense of loss for the displaced person. Like any kind of serious loss, this also leads to feelings of *grief.* The classic stages of grief, especially those of denial, anger, and depression, play a significant role in the experiences of those undergoing displacement. Fortunately, since most preachers also serve in a pastoral role, they have both training and experience in ministering to grieving people. Such preachers can use that expertise by viewing preaching amid displacement as a cross-cultural challenge to enable hearers to do the necessary work of grieving. In order to specify how preaching might accomplish this more readily, let us consider a broader and more basic goal for any work with those facing displacement.

Psychologists generally argue that, although displaced persons must find ways to separate from their previous settings in order to adapt to a new environment, some connection with the former situation is also important. If we think of the displaced person's former setting and new setting (whether in terms of locale, time, or belonging) as two different cultures, we can profitably use W. J. Berry's categories of acculturation to understand several coping options. Referring specifically to immigrants (locale displacement), Berry noted that they tend to adapt to a new place using one of four strategies. First, they may *integrate* themselves, continuing to identify and be involved with their former culture as well as the culture of the new setting. Second, they may *assimilate* themselves, identifying solely with culture of the new setting and completely relinquishing their ties to the former culture. Third, they may *separate* themselves, being involved exclusively in the traditional values of the former setting and having little or no interaction with members of the new culture. Fourth, they may *marginalize* themselves, rejecting both their former culture as well as that of the new setting.

These four strategies are listed in a descending order of usefulness for displaced persons, with integration being the most desirable and marginalization the least so. We should note that some researchers argue that a strategy of assimilation can be as effective as one of integration in certain cases. A strategy of separation raises problems because it focuses attention almost completely on the former setting and the possibility of return. People who cope in this fashion miss home desperately. They are obsessed with thoughts about it and continue to live mentally in their old environment. A strategy of marginalization is clearly viewed as being the most harmful. In this reactive and insulated approach aimed at self-protection, the displaced person in fact loses any real hope of a supportive culture, whether old or new.

Since the chief distinguishing feature of the frame of displacement is that it undercuts culture, Berry's remarks can helpfully clarify the cross-cultural challenge it presents to preaching. Unlike the other cultural frames of ethnicity, beliefs, and even class, displacement provides no worldview to call home. For this reason, the preacher's central task in this case is to assist people in rebuilding a culture. When preachers are aware of and attentive to displacement as a cultural frame, they have a distinctive opportunity to assist those who are suffering its effects. A preacher can aid hearers to rebuild a culture by crafting sermons that contribute to integrating the former culture with the new. Later in this chapter we will hear examples of the preaching strategies our interviewees used to help displaced persons integrate their differing and, at times, conflicting worlds. For now, however, we turn to those same voices to gain further insights into what characterizes the displaced among whom we preach.

Group Characteristics

Displacement represents a special obstacle to understanding the group characteristics of our hearers because it undermines the group-forming capacities of culture itself. To be sure, it also bears limited similarities to other cultural frames mentioned in this book. Like class, displacement represents an internalized, socially reinforced cultural reality whose impact may not be especially welcome. As with socioeconomic situations, therefore, ignoring the fact of displacement only worsens its potentially negative effects. Like ethnicity and beliefs, displacement requires some measure of intentional, participatory effort. The difference, of course, is that the ultimate aim of such effort is to overcome displacement rather than preserve it.

These similarities aside, however, displacement is at heart culturally corrosive. How, then, can we even speak about group characteristics for those whose central experience (in this case) is a loss of group and the things that contribute to distinctive cultural character? We realize that the frame of displacement imposes an artificial group identity on those it includes. Even so, those we interviewed who regularly encounter such people did in fact name three ways that culturally corrosive displacement shapes those lives. As a whole, displaced persons are set apart by their hidden wounds, perilous journeys, and special bonds. Each of these characteristics gives us a richer sense of the inner contours of those who hear our preaching.

Hidden Wounds

Although it might appear somewhat disheartening as a starting point, interviewees reminded us that displacement is basically invisible. Even to those directly affected by it (like Vanessa at the outset of this chapter), it is easily overlooked because it seems to lack evident substance and scale beyond the individual. As a private psychosocial wound like grief or depression, the effects of displacement can therefore easily remain hidden from others. One ironic outcome is that those suffering displacement may never recognize the many others around them who are in the very same plight. Feelings of isolation and rejection are heightened while, at the same time, available social resources for expressing and addressing displacement remain unused.

If these hidden wounds are characteristic for many of those who are displaced (whether they realize it for themselves or not), then preachers have a distinctive opportunity to draw this reality into the open and make it visible. Interviewees pointed out the importance of knowing what was specifically happening in the lives of those who faced significant and disorienting cultural change. Attentiveness therefore becomes the challenge for the preacher. Toward this end, experienced pastors suggested several concrete approaches.

Given what was said in previous chapters about regular involvement in the lives of parishioners, there is no surprise in learning that interviewees spoke of *visiting* as essential. One denominational judicatory official who now oversees ministry to recent immigrants from Mexico underscored this point.

> One of the first things, the important things to know is to at least have some knowledge as to where these people come from and what their life experience has been in regards to their immigration status—perhaps how they have grown up, the work they have done, the struggles in life, family life, values. All that, I think, is very important for the Anglo pastor to consider in preaching or sharing the gospel with the Hispanic community. And one of the things that is expected of the pastor that has a large number of Hispanic folks is visitation.

Although this advice relates directly to groups displaced from a locale, the same guidance surely fits in cases where the displacement is related to time or belonging.

An inner-city pastor working with a wide range of immigrants in his parish suggested there was more at stake with visiting than simply building better awareness of the displaced.

> You are looked on to do so many different things, from helping people understand, to advocating for them with Immigration and Naturalization, to finding jobs, to looking for housing—helping people just meet daily needs. I mean, they look to the church to do that and the pastor to do that. You embody the justice and the gospel that is spoken on Sundays. So I think, you know, the key for preaching is you have to be in people's homes and people's lives. Visitation is essential.

Note the implications in these remarks that bear upon both the displaced and our preaching. If displacement produces, among other things, a degrading loss of self-worth, then pastoral visits become a kind of "first preaching" by which dignity is reaffirmed and justice reasserted. Moreover, visiting puts flesh on the gospel in a living encounter of care and support long before it is actually announced from the pulpit.

Our informants surely did not idealize the potentials for visiting. One pastor of a church with Korean immigrant members spoke of a basic challenge, since her newly arrived members often held down several jobs in order to support an extended family. "I find visiting more difficult than I had in the past," she remarked, but then added, "so I'm trying to connect through the children in school sometimes, hearing some of the stories there, and trying to be around when parents and grandparents pick up kids and drop them off." When adjustment strains the lives of displaced persons, visiting requires creative approaches and a willingness to meet in alternative ways.

Having opened up a connection into the lives of displaced persons is only a starting point. Understanding the hidden wounds of such people requires active *questioning*, which those we interviewed described in two ways. On the one hand, some spoke of a kind of imaginative, empathetic inquiry through which people give voice to the changes they have faced. Referring to forms of displacement related to time, one pastor described this strategy.

> Well, one of the main things is helping them make sense of the present through the past—helping their past understand the present. So perhaps one of the biggest techniques you can use is to be nostalgic. For example, ask them, "How did you used to do this?" or "What did you used to do for Lent?" Stuff like that. And if you listen carefully, you begin to hear a kind of sadness over the way things used to be done, and now they're not. And you can take that and let it become the key to interpret their situation today.

What is striking is that this kind of conversation is far from passive. It calls for a lively awakening of the memories and feelings of the person who is displaced, drawing that individual into an activity he or she is solely competent to perform.

On the other hand, since displacement can include profound feelings of meaninglessness (recall, for example, how those who assimilate end up rejecting their former culture), a yet more active approach may be needed. Some respondents called for a kind of questioning alert to directly conveying value to prior traditions that were being forgotten or suppressed. A priest whose parish included a dazzling array of recently immigrated ethnic groups asserted, "People have many traditions, and sometimes they don't reflect on them, and you have to say that they *are* important, and you can be here and *still* have them." He specifically looked for these neglected practices and values and then intentionally highlighted their importance to the person being visited. Not incidentally, such examples were soon to show up in a homily as well.

Such insights into the hidden wounds of displaced persons are not to be hoarded but used. This use takes the form of *naming* what has been learned through visiting and questioning. This might seem like a peculiar topic within our specific concern to identify ways of being attentive to hidden wounds. Indeed, it seems more accurately to be a preaching strategy addressed later in this chapter. Our purpose here, however, is that naming rounds out the task of attentiveness, testing our understanding by holding us accountable to others. We cannot know whether we have adequately attended to their displacement without declaring that reality back to them, indicating that we have heard their experience and, by doing so, honored it.

Such naming needs to be, in the first instance, highly specific. Interviewees reminded us that no one, displaced or otherwise, appreciates having his or her distinctiveness reduced to generic terms. A pastor we met served a congregation with several first-generation Japanese immigrants who came to America just prior to the Second World War. They felt an enduring sorrow due both to cultural changes and their later treatment in America. These facts were true for many Japanese Americans, however, not just those in the congregation. What solidified a close relationship with these members was naming back to them a core experience that had touched them all: the loss of a neighborhood YWCA started by these same immigrants but seized from them during the war years. The highly specific naming of this loss conveyed that this pastor now understood their wounds.

Naming specific hidden wounds is only part of the story, however. The entire task paradoxically includes placing these specifics within a larger framework, renaming them in terms of their psychosocial significance. A displaced person experiencing some particular crisis of meaning or erosion of self-worth may never have heard that these feelings are not crazy. Naming includes confronting the isolating myth that one's situation is idiosyncratic. Through such a process of renaming, those who suffer from displacement learn a vocabulary for what their experiences mean that links them to the wounds of others. By knowing that loneliness, numbness, despair, and all the rest are part of the package of displacement, attentive preachers can anticipate these feelings in what they hear from parishioners and name these in broader terms so that their significance can be realized. Obviously, naming and renaming then become a basis for later preaching strategies in which we say in public what was formerly private, yet in a way that preserves personal dignity.

Perilous Journeys

Since displacement involves moving from a customary setting, it is only natural for us to characterize those seen through that frame as a group on a journey. That metaphor, as it turns out, is in fact a useful one according to our informants. Whether someone feels homesick, nostalgic, or alienated, there is a sense of being in motion from one reality to another, enduring a transitional existence while perpetually waiting to arrive. Because this journey is also disruptive and disorienting, it is therefore fraught with peril.

One imperiling feature is the kind and amount of *baggage* that accompanies the trip. Still speaking metaphorically, of course, baggage refers to the stuff of life that the displaced bring from a former setting that has *not* been lost but instead bears upon and even burdens them in the new. The Japanese Americans we mentioned just above are a case in point. Their pastor remarked about a perception these immigrants carry yet today that serves as just such baggage.

> In the case of the first generation, there's an ambivalence about Japan that continues into the second generation, too. Japanese in Japan are a very xenophobic group, and they have tended to look at Japanese who have left Japan as somehow having failed. They couldn't make it in their own country, and so they had to leave. They're either looked at as poor cousins or even a lower level of life. For the first-generation Japanese, this was very potent. Though they may have come and brought tremendous skills and energy and what not over here, they still have the sense that they are looked down on by Japanese in the homeland. That sense also continues in the second generation. They are ambivalent because they have one foot in American culture and one foot in Japanese culture. And then they know that when they meet Japanese from Japan, they're looked down on. But the third generation doesn't seem to be aware of that.

Of particular interest are the generational differences in this example. Those who directly experienced displacement also felt the greater weight of this baggage. Although actual contact with Japan was severely curtailed after immigration, the values from that setting were internalized and still mattered far from the homeland. By contrast, a later generation that integrated or even assimilated seemed not to be burdened at all.

Baggage can be affected by more than the recentness of a move or the internalization of values. The very reason one is displaced can also create its own kind of baggage. In thinking through the members of his congregation, a pastor from Florida remembered one group in particular. "We do have some folks that feel that they are displaced. We have some Cuban exiles, and they make sure that you understand that they are in exile and that the only reason they are here is because Castro is still in Cuba. And if he's gone, he dies, if he's shot, they may go back. That's been thirty years, but they still feel that they are here in exile, not by choice." Here we see an example of alienation with a vengeance, the result of a displacement of belonging. For these Cubans, the sense of forced expulsion imposes a duty to preserve former traditions and retain cultural identity in hopes of eventual return, no matter how distant or unrealistic that might be.

A pastor working in the Latino community in the San Francisco Bay area took a somewhat different spin on the topic. In this case, *elective* immigration for economic gain sometimes produced a baggage that *forced* expulsion did not.

> First of all, the concept of them moving to the States was to be here for no more than five years, make enough money, then move back to Puerto Rico and buy a home and live happily thereafter. There was never any sense of belonging or creating roots here in the States, because their idea was moving back to Puerto Rico. The new immigration, though, that is moving in from Latin America or South America—some of them have come over here for political reasons, so therefore they need to be a little more stable here in the States, and they want to make this their homeland.

In any case, it is plain that the reasons for leaving can shape the willingness to integrate into a new situation or separate from it. For similar reasons, we can easily imagine varying responses to displacement tied to time. No wonder resistance or hostility surface when change sweeps through someone's life in a sudden and uncontrollable way.

A journey is more than just the baggage we bring, of course. It also includes some sort of route. For those who journey through displacement, however, there has been *hardship* along the way. Many of us would be likely to attend to displaced persons as if their present situation were what mattered most. Our interviewees pointed out, however, that the long trek from a former setting up to now could well be filled with character-shaping and character-distorting experiences. Particularly when cruelty or injustice have marked the way so far, people are understandably dubious about the goodness of life or bright hope for the future. We need not belabor this, since the attentive preacher will already know (through visiting, questioning, and naming) the many obstacles that displaced persons have faced. Instead, we only join our interviewees in emphasizing that whether people can move beyond displacement, let alone hear and trust what we preach, is strongly affected by the kinds of challenges they endured long before we met them. Effective cross-cultural preachers simply assume these hardships exist.

A final point implied within the metaphor of a journey is the idea of reaching some *destination*. What makes the journey perilous for displaced persons is that this goal can appear elusive and even unattainable. Compounded by feelings of powerlessness and isolation, it is easy for such people to lose hope and embrace despair. For this very reason, experienced preachers pointed out the need to help a displaced person reclaim a vision, not simply of where the journey began, but also where it will end up. One pastor put it this way:

> We need to have a creative tension between affirming our origins and affirming our destinations. Although it's good for us to remember the places from which we came, in reality sometimes it's a trap that forces people to stay in their own place always. They never live here because in their minds they are back in Venezuela or Peru or wherever. So proper, good pastoral preaching will always have a sense of direction, will always have a sense of "God is fashioning something new."

Note that the effort is not to predict some particular goal, but instead to recover a sense of purpose and hope. It is hopeful to hear that the journey of displacement is not agonizingly endless but can reach its proper aim. The particular gift of the preacher is then to declare that this aim is shaped not by human effort but by God.

One distinctive way we can elicit this destination from and for displaced persons is to speak of it as a people rather than a location or experience. Amid disruptive change, people can be reminded that their journey's end is a community. Knowing this, the preacher may have special occasion to build connections to that new community. An interviewee in New York state described to us her realization that all of her parishioners had been immigrants at some point past.

> The Euro-American part of this congregation is historically an immigrant population, as is the Korean population. And in some ways I've seen some of the goal as making the connection to some of the similarities in their stories, and God's presence in their lives in different ways yet similar ways. I've been so struck by some similarities of some of our seniors to some of our newer Korean immigrants. We have one young woman whose father had been a pharmacist in Korea during wartime, and we have one senior whose father had been a pharmacist in Germany during wartime. Their stories of family reaching out to help heal the community are almost identical stories.

In this simple coincidence and others like it, this pastor sensed a common bond among the members that became a healing connection for the most recently displaced among them. Her preaching offered a destination for these members with one another and in God. She continued, "A part of the preaching that I do, a part of the gospel message, is that we all find a home together. Although geographically we may all be displaced, this is a place that gives us some stability in the midst of not being at home." The destination we can declare to others is the one we have together as the body of Christ.

In her foundational work *On Death and Dying,* Elisabeth Kübler-Ross identified the now familiar stages of denial, anger, bargaining, depression, and acceptance. She and others have been quick to point out, however, that those who are dying do not necessarily face such stages in the same order, duration, or intensity. We wish to say something similar about the perilous journey of displacement. Our interviewees spoke of three potent elements affecting this journey that we have labeled baggage, hardship, and destination. These are not, however, a predictable process through and beyond the journey of displacement. Instead, the significance of each element and the interplay between the three can help us better understand why a displaced person has become marginalized, separated, assimilated, or integrated along the way. We intend these as diagnostic tools not simply for pastoral care, but particularly to guide our decisions about what and how to preach among the displaced.

Special Bonds

As with our treatment of other cultural frames elsewhere in this book, so again we note here that there is no monolithic group character to those who are displaced. This was already clear when we described different kinds of displacement tied to locale, time, and belonging, as well as the differing rates at which it can be experienced, from evolutionary to revolutionary. Beyond this, however, is a cluster of other factors that refines and completes our picture of group characteristics for the displaced. These factors help to account for the wide and often confounding variations among those who might otherwise be considered to be quite similar.

Chief among these factors is the *generation* in which one has been displaced, a matter already hinted at in quotations earlier in this chapter. Obviously, this distinction applies most directly to those displaced from a locale. We must clarify, however, that it does not refer primarily to chronological age or rank in a family structure. Instead, using the example of immigration, one's generation may be that of an adult at the time of a move, a person born in the homeland but reaching maturity in the new setting, or someone born and raised entirely in the new setting. This generational differentiation into three or, by some reckonings, four groups affects the experience of almost every immigrant group mentioned by our informants, whether that displacement was in the recent or distant past. (Although our interviewees never discussed this directly, we can easily imagine analogous "generations" in experiencing displacement tied to time or belonging.)

Whether speaking of immigrants from the Eastern or Southern Hemispheres in more recent years or from western Europe a century before that, we were repeatedly told of a deep divide between the earlier and later generations. While the former hold to customary ways and tend to live in enclaves, the latter are often eager to fit into the new setting. Paradoxically, this eagerness is sometimes encouraged by the earlier generations who rely on their offspring to be culture brokers in the new setting. This is not without its own painful adjustment, however, as when the American-born children of immigrants must advocate for their parents and grandparents in medical, social service, or labor situations—a role they may not be prepared to handle emotionally. When these children become adults, more-over, resentment sometimes erupts at essentially being forced to forego treasured ties to a homeland.

Most striking of all about this generational characteristic of displacement, how-ever, is how it creates unusual alliances beyond family or ethnicity. A pastor familiar with several Asian immigrant groups over the course of many years remarked:

> This third Japanese American generation has a distinct culture. They were encour-aged by their parents to become primarily professional people, and to succeed even to a greater extent than the second-generation parents. But then they have this link with the Chinese Americans who are born in this country, third- and fourth-generation Chinese Americans, because they have experienced the same concerns and issues that the Japanese do while growing up and going to school and getting jobs and so forth. They have a link between one another that is greater than the links to their parents' generation.

This connection with others by generation rather than ethnic homeland is not limited to the later generations, as another pastor added:

> We are generally looking at Koreans who are mid-teens to early twenties. As they grow up, they want to be American. But in many respects, their parents are trying to maintain the culture of the homeland. And that mirrors the immigration experi-ence here a couple of generations ago, because this congregation still has a good number of first-generation Germans who came over in the forties and fifties. What they were trying to do, too, was maintain their tradition and maintain their culture.

All of this recalls our earlier remarks about hardships (or the lack thereof) in the journey of displacement. Our interviewees clarified that what unites people in displacement may be less about the new or former setting and more about the ex-periences along the way. On generational grounds, such experiences may lead to feeling closer to those from distant lands than those within one's household.

Closely related to these generational experiences were two other factors affect-ing displaced persons. One of these was proficiency with *language*. Since language use forms a basic social device for inclusion and exclusion, feeling alienated from or accepted in one's surroundings is a natural (and intended) by-product. It is in-triguing, however, that linguistic skill, whether in the language of a former setting or a new one, may stand in an unusual tension with the generation of displacement. For example, we were told of first generation immigrants whose deftness in English in no way moderated their staunch support of a homeland or resistance to integrating into American society. By contrast, one interviewee who was himself the grandchild of immigrants but born in New York always sensed he was treated differently because of his fluency in his grandparent's tongue. Although he claimed America as his home, the role of language provoked an enduring sense of exile. Our larger point is that language preferences and multilingual ability can become one more factor affecting how displacement is perceived over the long run. We heard similar comments about time displacement in reference to those who felt they were now left "speaking a foreign language" because of recent cultural and social changes.

The remaining factor that can create a special bond characterizing displaced persons is that of *piety*. Religious beliefs (the focus of the next chapter) often provide crucial cultural reinforcement in the face of corrosive displacement. In particular, our respondents described the perceived importance of the religious community as a microcosm by which a former setting could be maintained or a new one introduced and embraced. Seen through the frame of displacement, this gives a new perspective on why some congregations are so resistant to altering even the smallest of traditions. For those feeling displaced from the mainstream of time or belonging, church may well be the only safe haven in a gathering storm.

Piety provides a shelter amid other kinds of displacement as well. In a congregation with many different ethnic subgroups, one priest pointed out the large number of religious practices through which the cultural identity of immigrants was maintained. "Currently where I serve, we have seventeen different Latino communities within that congregation. Each one of them not only feels important, but they feel that if we do not have one of their own expressions of popular devotion in the congregation through a big celebration once a year that their own communal identity is lost. So we need to be very sensitive to those expressions." Of course, this is nothing new. Thinking about both present-day immigrants and those from an earlier period, another pastor commented how all these parishioners have consistently acted as if "the church represented the homeland." By contrast, he added, "the younger people just see the church very differently." What people expect from the church can therefore become both a product of displacement and a contributor to how it is experienced.

Preaching Strategies

As an anti-cultural experience, displacement strips us of what ordinarily helps orient and guide our lives. Knowing this, we can already see that preaching involves a kind of redirecting. If we can agree that certain forms of dealing with displacement are simply unhealthy, then our aim should ultimately be to point toward an integration that honors both the former situation and the new. Beyond promoting mere psychosocial adjustment, however, the preacher can distinctively declare a Christ who knows our most hidden wounds and perilous journeys and offers a special bond regardless of the present circumstances.

Redirecting the displaced through preaching means first rebuilding a world they can inhabit. We seek through our words to restore what has been lost, from a sense of home to a horizon for hope. The strategies offered here again derive inductively from our interviews and suggest how others have met this rebuilding and redirecting challenge. We gather their advice under the headings of constructive forms, parallel images, expressive models, and later effects.

Constructive Forms

We have already mentioned the special bond that language provides in the midst of displacement, let alone (in chapter 2) its role in reinforcing ethnic character. Such remarks belong within a larger sociolinguistic insight that the words we choose help establish group boundaries and maintain group identity. Linguistic variation by register (what we say) and dialect (how we speak) become discernable social markers of who belongs and who does not. If we apply this metaphorically to preaching among the displaced, we can begin to sense the immense social potential of sermons either to undermine or reconstruct. Regarding the former possibility, a pastor with many parishioners facing class and ethnic upheaval offered a warning. "My perspective is that everyone needs a sense of place. And as long as people have a sense of place, then what's going on, participating in change or what have you, does not have the same threat and the fear isn't as big. And I'm not willing with my words to undermine people's place unless I also assume some responsibility in helping open another place for people to have." The caution was not blindly to preserve some status quo but instead to realize both the destructive impact of thoughtless speech and the constructive possibilities inherent in effective cross-cultural preaching.

As a starting point, this involves a self-conscious effort to *avoid verbal distance* through our vocabulary and syntax. This is an especially challenging task for preachers because it asks us to rethink the shorthand ways of speaking we have learned through academic books and formal education. As examples of verbally distancing language, our respondents referred to theologically dense concepts or abstractions having little ordinary use today (such as "righteousness" or "justification") as well as obscure and ancient terms familiar only within limited ecclesial circles (such as Agnus dei or Nunc dimittis). Such shorthand indeed remains useful as the technical language of a specific discipline, but its unintended effect when used in preaching is to push people away. Interviewees were by no means advocating a "dumbing down" of the substance of the sermon. In fact, they saw great importance in drawing deeply from the reservoir of profound truths or ritual actions to which these technical terms refer. What was distinctive about their preaching, however, was that they had learned to do this without a lazy appeal to customary in-house language. By avoiding what might further disorient their already displaced hearers, they were clearing a common space on which to build.

Upon that foundation, these same preachers then sought to *erect verbal assurances*. By this, we mean that the form and style of language helped to keep listeners on track and oriented to the message itself. As an overarching device, interviewees frequently pointed out the value of narrative—advice that appears several times elsewhere in this book. One pastor's basic approach with her Laotian immigrant members was simply "to tell stories within the context of the sermon. Even though they say 'teach me,' the way Laotian folks teach each other is that they tell stories." Her brief comment is important first because it indicates that stories are not devices for sermonic entertainment but substantive vehicles for serious work. Moreover, her words imply a special value for narrative in relation to displacement, since it may at times serve as a bridging form of speech, both familiar from the former setting and relevant in the new. Narratives also construct an assurance in one final way. Their commonality can, as another preacher put it, "both draw people in and draw people together." The narrative world becomes a new home for the displaced, however briefly, and one they inhabit alongside others in the community of the faithful.

This timeworn advice about narrative is not the end of the matter, however. Other forms of language were mentioned that also construct verbal assurances for the displaced hearer. Repetition was one of these. Drawing upon discoveries during a previous pastorate in a multicultural congregation, a respondent said that this had become a standard device in his preaching today in a largely immigrant community.

> I have them repeat a phrase. This is something I learned in African American services, where you might say, "Because Jesus rose from the dead," and they'll respond with "We can live forever." So I say at the beginning of a message that I'm going to be using a certain phrase every once in a while, and when I say it I want you to raise your hand and say this response. Then I'll have them try it, and then practice it again with a little more emphasis. And it's a way in which they can participate more in the sermon, too.

A good bit of wisdom is packed into this remark, for repetitive devices like this accomplish several things. They heighten mutual participation in the sermon by creating a rhythm of expectation. Hearers adopt a posture of readiness for their cues and thus are subtly taught how and for what they should listen. The responses are also quickly memorized and thus portable, becoming a way to carry the sermon home and into the coming week. Not least of all, repetition becomes a kind of handrail through the course of the sermon, orienting the listener in moving from one thing to the next. Interviewees suggested many different forms of repetition beyond the call-and-response method familiar in black preaching. Apart from seeking verbal responses, for example, the preacher might use a brief refrain line at key points in the sermon or a parallel sentence structure (think of the famous "we cannot dedicate, we cannot consecrate, we cannot hallow this ground" from the Gettysburg Address) as other repetitive forms that build verbal reassurance.

Another way language can reassure displaced persons involves something we ordinarily do in conversations: ask questions. Note, however, that this is not the unhelpful posing of ponderous rhetorical questions to which no serious response is expected. The concrete purpose is instead to monitor how the hearers are engaging the sermon and to adjust accordingly, if necessary. "Your preaching has to be open-ended and needs to be testing back-and-forth to check out perceptions," advised one pastor from Chicago. "I feel much better when I know halfway through my sermon that people know what I'm talking about instead of waiting to the very end and wondering if they got anything." Responses to this kind of testing vary by group, of course, from verbal replies to more subtle nods or looks of puzzlement. This strategy calls for the preacher flexibly to react to the information received. The larger benefit, however, is that of building both mutuality with the hearers and a basis for their deeper participation.

Other respondents were quick to warn that verbal devices that were too open-ended could become disorienting and even counterproductive. While testing of listener perception may be valuable at some points in the sermon, at others it can confound and thus undercut the very assurance the preacher intends. An example from preaching in a prison, certainly a situation of displacement, was instructive. "I throw questions in the middle, but I wouldn't just end it like that. Stylistically I don't end it like that because they would be confused. The code of communication is to end with something very concrete, so they say, 'Ah, yes, this is what it's about; this is what we got today.' And it's got to be much more explicit here than when I go somewhere else." This interesting observation suggests that the circumstance of displacement may create a special need to be more overt about closure. Without robbing the hearers of a participatory role in the sermon, preachers can assure displaced persons by crafting a fitting summary that appropriately hands over the sermon.

As a final remark, we heard once again about the importance of speech rate and visual aids, but this time in terms of the assurance they offered. Especially in light of wide generational differences and language competencies that characterize displaced persons, slower speech becomes a simple yet crucial means for those who struggle with English to stay engaged with a sermon. In a related way, we were told that judicious use of visual devices could sometimes be an assuring enhancement to the preaching. Moreover, such devices created a common ground where the very youngest and oldest persons present could meet through the sermon and participate together.

Parallel Images

In some respects, the foregoing advice about constructive forms can be understood as an effort to combat the isolating effects of displacement. By using language that avoids distance and erects assurances, the preacher seeks to bind hearers together in a common sermonic experience. Forms of speech, however, are not the only way to do this. Even more potent, we learned of many substantive references that helped to name the situation of displaced persons so they could find a new home within a faithful community. Our respondents made use of a large number of analogies typically drawn from scripture, images that powerfully evoked some kind of parallel to the experiences of displacement. So vast and rich were these parallel images that we can only touch on a few here, categorizing them into two basic types: figures and processes.

Figure analogies referred to individuals in the Bible who had themselves known some kind of displacement. Often these figures were themselves part of a rejected group, of which there is no shortage in scripture. Among those most frequently cited were Abraham (in departing from Haran, Genesis 12), the Canaanite woman (Matthew 15), the Good Samaritan (Luke 10), and the woman at the Sychar well (John 4), although others were used and are not difficult to imagine. In general, these parallels were selected because the figures involved were either forced to leave home or alienated in their present setting, an obvious analogy to the leaving and adjustment being faced by hearers who were now displaced. They were quite flexibly used, moreover, to name experiences ranging from homesickness to nostalgia to alienation. As we shall see, however, this was not their only purpose.

One distinctive figure not mentioned above was the frequent reference to Jesus himself as embodying the experience of displacement. From his birth in a place that was no human habitation, to his family's flight as refugees, to his rejection within his own homeland, to his very ministry as a wandering teacher and healer, Jesus becomes a particularly potent example of being a refugee in unity with the displaced. As with the use of other parallel biblical figures, then, the idea in referencing Jesus in this way is to convey that displaced persons are in good company and their plight is intimately known by God.

This is not the final aim of this parallel with Jesus, however, for respondents did not simply regard him as another hapless victim. Although displaced, Jesus' life had a saving and liberating aim that includes all others who are displaced. As one person put it:

These people are so isolated. They feel a disconnectedness because they are not at home, or because they don't have a home to go back to if they leave here. But Jesus was going from place to place, too, and doing what? Loving and teaching and going toward the goal of his life. These people—their life is going to be homeless in all sorts of levels, but in that aloneness they can see Jesus did that and had a goal in mind. The big reality in their life may still be that aloneness, homelessness, but they can have a goal of love in their life and feel loved by someone who had that kind of life. It's something that they listen to.

The analogy of Jesus' own journey is therefore used not simply to parallel contemporary, painful experiences of displacement, but also to point to the cross through which abundant life is restored. Another pastor even named this parallel as posing a critical question to the displaced. "What does Jesus say about the Son of Man having no place to lay his head? Are they then willing to understand this being off balance as the appropriate posture to be more vulnerable and open to God?" In larger scope, then, the figure of Jesus, when used as a parallel image in preaching, serves the twin purposes of identifying with the plight of the displaced and challenging it.

These twin purposes can be seen not only with reference to Jesus but also in relation to the wide range of other biblical figures mentioned earlier. Indeed, it seems that one of the strengths of using parallel figures is their very ability to convey more than one message about displacement, including a message that might be rather difficult to hear. Referring to a sermon in a congregation with many immigrant members, a pastor recalled speaking of a biblical figure in just this way.

Many of the people here are more recent immigrants, so the whole issue of immigration is an important thing. So I talk about the Canaanite woman and how she was ignored, and you know everybody is on the same wavelength. But then I say, "You know, she's also an obnoxious person," and we all know obnoxious people. They can all think of a person they don't like who bugs them a lot. And then I ask how many times we turn people off because we think their behavior is obnoxious or because they are from a different culture. In this community, you deal with tensions between African American and Latino. So we're talking about that and what it means that the church is a refuge—a refuge for people in need, for foreigners—and how you live with the pressures that try to divide us up.

By providing a fuller view of the Canaanite woman, her behavior becomes the basis for an honest and perhaps more troubling self-recognition on the part of the displaced. Other biblical texts present an ensemble of figures with whom hearers can identify. A preacher we interviewed employed this strategy in his urban church where class and ethnic variations were wide and concerns about dislocation were persistent. He invited his hearers to adopt each role in the Good Samaritan parable in turn (victim, robbers, priest, Levite, Samaritan, and innkeeper) to examine not simply their own sense of displacement but also how this might be broken open and given new direction and purpose.

The dual message implicit in parallel figures can move hearers not only from identification to challenge, as we have just seen, but also from identification to hope. The figure of Abraham was used this way in one congregation with a regular turnover of members and a pervasive sense of transience and disruption. The preacher began by noting the upheaval produced in Abraham's life when God commanded him to leave home, but then she noted something more.

> So God sent Abraham "to a land I will show you," and he was a displaced individual. But he was sent by God to a new land, to have a new life, to begin a new people. Abraham became new, became renewed in that new place. We may be displaced, but to a land that God has chosen, to find ourselves there. The Israelites moved to a new land, and then they became a new people. It was there that they found themselves. They were further defined by God.

Radical disorientation does not become the final word. Instead, the parallel shows a displacement whose end is renamed by God.

This last quotation also hints at another kind of parallel figure. Our informants sometimes used texts that permitted their hearers to identify with a group in scripture rather than a specific individual. Thus, hearers might identify with the Israelites as a group both beleaguered by change yet part of God's promise. In certain settings of displacement, however, the group with whom hearers identify may be surprising. Native Americans who have been repeatedly displaced since the days of European conquest, for example, tend to see more of a parallel with the Canaanites than with Israel. Telling such stories from the underside can be a powerful device, however, when our aim among the displaced is to tell the truth of unresolved injustice. The larger point is that biblical figures, whether individuals or groups, remain stubbornly multivalent. Using them in any setting of displacement requires carefully considering how they might speak in dramatically different ways.

Process analogies are the other category of parallel images mentioned by our interviewees. Although these often also imply a parallel figure of some sort (especially the journeys of Israel or the struggles of early Christians), the emphasis is more on an action or activity with which hearers are invited to make a connection. Like figure analogies, the preacher's initial purpose is for displaced persons to see their own challenges in parallel to some process presented in scripture. Images of enslavement (Exodus 1), wilderness wandering (Exodus 16), exilic sorrow (Psalm 137), and persecution (2 Corinthians 4) were frequently mentioned by our interviewees as such parallel processes. By identifying with these processes, displaced persons once again could recognize that they were not alone or crazy for feeling as they did, and that, moreover, their story was inscribed in a larger biblical framework.

At the same time, however, process analogies served more than this limited purpose. The preachers we interviewed built upon this first set of connections to create a further parallel between the experience of displaced persons and key redemptive processes in scripture. Many of these can be viewed as forms of liberation, ranging from the exodus itself (Exodus 12–15) to prophetic calls for freedom and justice (Isaiah 61 and Luke 4). Our interviews revealed that process analogies tend to be used to support a general sermonic theme, in contrast with figure analogies that remain anchored to a particular text. The result is sometimes a pastiche of text references clustered around God's central aim to liberate, as one preacher demonstrated.

> Well, for instance, I'm just working on my sermon for Sunday right now. What I'm preaching on is where Jesus comes up and says in the Capernaum synagogue, you know, "The Spirit of the Lord is upon me—and today this has been fulfilled in your hearing." And I'm tying that in with the Jubilee in Leviticus and that whole sense of "When the horn sounds, you'll go home and be with your family." So on Sunday, I'll be talking about how that's what Jesus is coming to do, to sound the horn, telling us that one day we'll go home. And a large part of my proclamation will be that the horn has sounded, the jubilee has come, the future hope is a present reality. You will once again be able to go home.

In this case and others like it, the displaced are invited to see a specific vision of hope and then claim it as their own. One pastor enthusiastically spoke of just this matter in recalling how her immigrant listeners, "even when the text was read in English, just started shaking their heads and saying, 'Yeah! God is right there for me in all this!'"

One final feature of process analogies is that they are often just as capable of conveying dual messages as are figure analogies. A pastor offered this example:

> We use the word *pilgrimage* a lot, because these folks are on a pilgrimage. And we also use the word *sojourner,* like in the text we read yesterday about "a wandering Aramean was my ancestor." People really related to that, that we're all really sojourners together. I've got four people who are here right now without the proper papers and who have been a part of our congregation for the last eight years. So we preach about how we are all sojourners and what that means for hospitality.

The dual aspect of images like pilgrimage and sojourner is that, on the one hand, they speak the hard truth of displacement while, on the other, they point onward to a hope-filled community gathered into God. Another text used by a different preacher also provided an image with multiple messages.

For example, I preached on 1 Peter 2, talking about how the church is now home for all of us who are homeless. Some of us are here because we want to be or we were born here, and some of us are here like the people from South America who are political refugees from the wars that savaged the region in the 1980s. But now we are all here, and the church is called to be a temple made out of living stones, a spiritual house in which all of us, it doesn't matter where we came from, are fashioning a new people. We who were not a people are a people. We who had no home now have a home. We are now a holy priesthood. You have to understand that for many of us, the church is the only or the major support group.

This dual capacity to name both profound loss ("not a people") and communal vision ("a holy priesthood") shows the tremendous power these process images have to speak the whole truth to those who are displaced.

Expressive Models

By using the parallel images mentioned above, our interviewees tried to offer their hearers a biblical way of naming and renaming the experience of displacement. In addition to these images, however, stands a kind of expressive scriptural language that typically remains a neglected resource for this same kind of cross-cultural preaching. Here we refer less to *what* a biblical text mentions than *how* it works as a model for speaking. Our effort is still to provide language by which displaced persons can name their situation, but now in terms of form rather than content. We raised a similar topic in chapter 2 by identifying several speech genres that were highly effective given the characteristics of the frame of ethnicity. Here we highlight one further genre particularly germane to the frame of displacement: lament.

Out of pastoral motivations, Walter Brueggemann once separated the book of Psalms into three groups: songs of orientation, disorientation, and new orientation. While the first group affirms the order of creation and the last group shouts the surprise of new life, the middle group voices the haunting reality of disarray. These are the psalms of lament, both personal (such as Psalms 13, 35, and 86) and communal (such as Psalms 74, 79, and 137). To this biblical repertoire we should also add the painful dirges of Lamentations and the probing speeches of Job. The astute reader of scripture knows there is no shortage of such expressions of outrage and sorrow.

For some people, being brutally honest about pain, loss, and failure sounds like lack of trust in God, a scandal amid what Douglas John Hall once aptly coined "the officially optimistic society." For Brueggemann, however, lament is deeply faithful because it accurately names an aspect of human reality and then addresses that reality to God. "All things that can be spoken," he said, "can be spoken to God." In light of the anti-cultural power of displacement, it is nothing short of counter-cultural to preach with such an aim. These psalms and other texts like them speak the unspeakable in order to strengthen hearers to endure the unendurable—an effort decidedly against the grain in a society accustomed to numbness and denial.

Our particular interest in lament is not simply that it evokes the reality it names, but the way it does so. Claus Westermann long ago noted the broad two-part pattern that typifies the structure of lament psalms. First comes the *plea,* a complaint to God that begs redress of an intolerable situation. Such psalms do not view disorientation as a natural passage to which we must resign ourselves. Instead, they name a rupture in the covenant relationship that must be repaired. This is why such songs must be uttered to God within the faithful community. Second, following immediately upon the plea comes the *praise,* a song of gratitude again uttered to God. This surprising move is not based on hastily rushing to some easy answer. Instead, what leads to praise is the hard-fought realization that our plea has indeed been heard *even if the circumstances remain disorienting.* To utter a grievance before one with power to resolve it is already the beginning of freedom and hope.

Preaching amid the displaced gains a valuable model from this two-part pattern of lament in the psalms. The pattern first models a cry of injustice for those whose lives are in disarray. Indeed, if we are true to scripture, this cry will be made in terms that are vivid, imaginative, and shockingly bold. Beyond this, the pattern then models a gratitude that this cry can be uttered at all (because we are still able to speak) and absorbed into the reality of God (because it is made in the household of faith). To sing of the One who can bear our displacement is also the basis for restoration and the first step toward finding a trustworthy home.

Naturally, other expressive models can be imagined from forms of lament elsewhere in scripture. In the alphabetic acrostic pattern of Lamentations, for example, each verse in a chapter begins with a successive letter of the Hebrew alphabet. The overall effect is to force that lengthy cry through the narrow channel of an artificial literary device, like water unleashed through the narrow sluice of a dam. The result of this interplay is to confer yet more impressive force to the lament. Cross-cultural preaching could employ such insights to intensify what is said about displacement. Another expressive model would be the question-and-reply pattern of the exchanges between Job and his unhelpful friends. Preaching could use a similar device to model both the questioning of our plight and the inadequacy of any human response. Our larger point, of course, is that such models or others like them permit the displaced to hear their plight identified and given guidance even by the basic way we pattern our sermons.

Later Effects

The final preaching strategy garnered from our interviews can be stated rather briefly and may sound less homiletical than therapeutic. When it comes to the frame of displacement, however, the line between the two may indeed be over-stated. More frequently than when referring to the frames of ethnicity or class but about as frequently as with the frame of religious beliefs, preachers portrayed the sermon as but a first step in a much longer conversational process. For this reason, we close this chapter by highlighting the strategy of noticing the later effects of our preaching.

Although displacement is anti-cultural and requires moving people beyond as the appropriate pastoral aim, there is no serious possibility that the preaching event alone will be able to do this. At its best, of course, hearers will sense in effective preaching that their plight has been named and they have been equipped with a new set of images and expressions. Interviewees were quick to add that, instead of being the end of the matter, this only means that a future conversation has now been set in motion. The sermon itself is not finished (if it ever is) until the displaced themselves bring it to closure in light of their present needs.

Experienced preachers therefore learned to listen for the impact of their preaching in subsequent pastoral conversations. As anyone who has listened to sermon responses might suspect, our interviewees reported how many times a single image or expression evoked contradictory reactions within the same group of hearers. The earlier example in which the Canaanite woman served as a figure of displacement is a case in point. Some of the displaced glimpsed in her a reflection of their outcast status, while others saw their own persistence, and still others acknowledged the way they had treated "obnoxious" outsiders. We do not mean that the Canaanite woman and other figures like her are merely scriptural Rorschach inkblots in which people see what they wish. Instead, when understood theologically such instances demonstrate the power of one and the same Word both to accuse and set free.

The whole truth of displacement, from loss to hope, can be conveyed through a single text or sermon. Discerning pastors we met listened for how people later reacted and what this might mean next. What they often learned was that the sermon was not yet over. Hearing one's pain accurately named and nothing more gave only a reason for despair. The sermon now had to be finished in private by speaking more richly of God's complete fidelity. Hearing one's actions fully convicted and nothing more gave only a rationale for paralysis. The sermon now had to be finished in private by giving occasion for confession and forgiveness. Effective preaching in settings of displacement sometimes demands a further intervention. It grows to completion through the office of the keys.

Like so many other tasks in public ministry, the effective exercise of such preaching makes our work more complex, not less. It demands in this case that, long after the sermon is done, the preacher continue to recognize its trajectory. This requires the ongoing effort to remain open to what others have heard and show our trustworthiness in so listening. Not incidentally, this underscores our earlier remarks in this chapter about the importance of visiting, in this case not as preparation for preaching but as follow-through. By pastoral conversation and consolation, our hearers receive a deeper encounter with the text and a greater opportunity to move beyond their displacement. Such pastoral work can also, of course, be valuable for sermons yet to come, further refining the issues still to be addressed.

5. The Frame of Beliefs

Susan was usually ready for anything, but one particular day even she was caught off guard. As part of the pastoral staff of a growing downtown congregation, she expected cultural diversity in many forms. The English-language worship service at which she preached was but one among others conducted each Sunday in Spanish, Finnish, Korean, and K'janobal (a Guatemalan dialect). She knew that even at the English service the people were a mix of ethnicities, classes, and kinds of dislocation or relocation. Unfamiliar faces were no surprise at worship, either. So when Susan saw several women with their children in attendance one Sunday, none of whom she had ever met, she was ready to welcome them warmly. The challenge they brought, however, took her totally by surprise.

Susan's sermon focused on baptism and made reference to the conversation in the gospel of John between Jesus and Nicodemus, that Sunday's assigned reading. Outspoken in her opposition to rebaptism, Susan criticized this practice for distorting what Jesus meant by being "born again." As she later remembered that morning, however, her critique did not remain unanswered.

> I was enthusiastic and humorous about how many born-again people there are in prison, especially at their parole hearings. I went on and on, giving a very skeptical look at the whole idea of being born again in the Pentecostal sense. At the end of the worship, one of the visiting women and her children shook hands with me at the door. She looked me right in the eyes and said in a solemn, almost angry way, "Being born again is what stopped me from trying to kill myself a second time." Not until later that week did I learn that, across the street from our church, two shelters for battered women had just opened. They were run by the Union Rescue Mission, so all of the women were required to attend a Christian service of their choice and bring back a bulletin to prove they attended. My worship service was the only one in English that was within walking distance from the shelter. She was stuck with me

for the next twelve Sundays of her program, and I had just battered her again in the sermon.

The visitor did indeed return the next Sunday, leading Susan to add, with irony, "The Holy Spirit still works, I guess." The quite different work of that same Spirit in this woman's life compared to Susan's, however, causes us to consider one final cross-cultural challenge to preaching. How can our preaching be heard by people whose religious worlds are so different from our own? To address this, we turn to the cultural frame of *beliefs*.

Susan's reflections set a course for ours in this chapter. First of all, we should notice the *proximity* of her encounter with alternative beliefs. While we naturally expect so-called "exotic" religious groups to differ widely from our own, Susan faced a chasm within Christianity, her own home. Such pieties and positions are often more difficult to address than those originating outside Christianity. The born-again visitor in this story was close to Susan's congregation in another way, as well: it was simply her only available option. Susan said she learned through this encounter that many people end up with a particular faith group not by choice but by chance or necessity, bringing their religious differences along for the ride.

This story also underscores the very different *purposes* embedded in our beliefs. Susan's preaching focused on religious concepts, their consistency and reasonableness. Beliefs do not always function this way for other people, however. We do not mean that their commitments merely mask profane motivations, but instead that religion can serve practical or nonrational ends as well. Some people are involved in religious groups for the sake of friendships, program benefits, therapy, healing, magical protection, and so forth. As for the woman who visited Susan's church, being born again represented nothing less than survival. Her case reminds us to ask not simply how the beliefs of others may differ but also why those beliefs are held at all.

Related to this, Susan's story demonstrates that we meet beliefs in their *particularity*. Religions are not primarily deposits of ideas or concepts but exist through actual people and practices. When Susan railed against being born again, she was confronted by a real person for whom that practice was deeply treasured. Susan was no longer dealing with an abstract theological claim. Her only authentic option was to engage this woman's commitments in all their specificity and concreteness. What is more, this incident did not pose theoretical questions that Susan could freely ponder in splendid isolation. As with other cross-cultural challenges to preaching, beliefs show us again the irreducible otherness of the neighbor.

This suggests a helpful direction for how preaching might attend to the cultural frame of beliefs. As with previous chapters, we will later collect our interviewees' insights about this frame under the broad headings of *group characteristics* and *preaching strategies*. For now, however, we must raise a prior concern about why preaching should bother with alternative religious claims and commitments in the first place. More to the point, how can Christian preaching do so without subverting either its own distinctive beliefs or those of another group? To answer this requires examining the nature of inter-religious *difference* and what it ultimately means to enter into *dialogue.*

Difference and Dialogue

Christians have often considered other religious traditions in two ways that are as distorted as they are dishonest. On the one hand, in an apparent effort at open-mindedness, we may regard other beliefs as simply alternative embodiments of the same religious essence that Christianity asserts. In their sincerity and quest for truth, believers from other religions are actually affirming Christian values unawares. Similarly, any distinctive or particular claims about Christianity are set aside in order to expose the underlying agreement between our beliefs and others. This approach presumes a peculiar kind of "bad faith" in which devout people of all stripes evidently do not really mean what they say, or at least not to an extent that produces substantive disagreement. Differences between Christianity and other religions are erased by being taken as imaginary.

On the other hand, in an apparent effort to preserve the purity of the gospel, we may regard other beliefs as completely at odds with anything that Christianity asserts. A charitable outlook toward believers from other religions certainly respects their choices and may even value their perspectives, but no more than this is possible. Other beliefs are judged inadequate or even defective when measured against the solitary standard of Christian truth. Differences between Christianity and other religions are erased, not because the differences are imaginary but because the veracity of other traditions is.

Both of these approaches, under which a surprising number of typical views can actually be subsumed, operate out of at least two flawed assumptions. First, they combine religious traditions into a single reality with a monolithic sameness we would never tolerate if the focus were instead on Christianity. Referring to many different religions as a single group, even in this chapter, is actually just another way of saying that we favor a particular religious perspective: our own. There is nothing wrong with this, of course, since Christianity is the tradition we cherish. It is unsatisfactory to leave the matter there, however, fusing all other traditions into a shapeless whole. Speaking of another religion requires the same nuance and specificity we would expect to be accorded to Christianity.

A second faulty assumption is that the approaches above remove the chance for any genuine encounter from the start. In both cases there are no truly alternative traditions to be faced, because those alternatives are either unreal (other religions are the same) or unworthy (other religions fall short). Beneath this assumption is a suppressed fear that actually to encounter another set of beliefs might mean that we will be changed. To contain this risk, we rule out in advance any possibility of encountering difference and with it any means for seriously engaging the religious traditions of others.

If preachers are to address the cross-cultural challenge represented by beliefs, neither of the approaches above will do. Our preaching will either be detached from other traditions or dismissive of our own. At heart, we seem to be hampered by an inadequate understanding of religious *difference* itself. By first taking a more rigorous look at four aspects of this kind of difference, we can then envision how our preaching might be a catalyst for dialogue in a diverse environment of beliefs.

Religious difference needs first to be understood as highly *variable*. Difference between specific groups is not a strict "yes or no" assessment, but instead a matter of degree relative to a given setting or encounter. Episcopalians in the South might have far less in common with Baptists than they do with Reform Jews, while the reverse might be the case in New England. Moreover, these distinctions may shift depending on whether the reason for the encounter is a service project or joint worship. Compounding differences due to situation are those due to time. Any religious tradition, even within itself, is dynamic and in motion, changing and developing in unpredictable ways. What once separated religious groups may later be bridged, while new events can expose opposing beliefs where none had previously been expressed. Religious difference is a fluid matter to be assessed by looking at specific settings and particular times.

Related to this is something to which we alluded earlier, that religious difference is *embodied*. In one sense, this means dealing with the lived practices and actual history of a group. A common danger is adopting a textbook view of other traditions that traces only their broadest contours in a necessarily generic portrayal. Reading papal encyclicals is certainly one way of understanding Roman Catholicism, but it hardly accounts for the distinctive rites and customs of the Polish Catholic parish down the street. This also serves to remind us that religious difference is embodied in actual human groups. As with other cultural frames, so also with beliefs we are dealing with groups that are not monolithic. That local Polish Catholic parish may consist of several subgroups that stand in significant theological tension with one another. Religious difference is a social reality to be assessed by looking at concrete actions and living adherents.

The opening anecdote of this chapter implied that religious difference is also *oriented*. For the born-again visitor in that story, beliefs were not an optional or value-added element but provided a means for her survival. This guiding role is crucial because what distinguishes a tradition may be more a matter of what it does than what it says. Gerd Baumann (see Suggested Readings) notes that religions should be seen like a sextant that determines one's position in relation to an ever-changing nighttime sky. Religion also orients in another way, by giving personal identity and social boundaries in times of threat. Severe religious disputes then result when ultimate and absolute claims define who we are and where we belong. Religious difference is a functional question to be assessed by looking at guidance offered and order conferred.

We should lastly underscore how religious difference is truly *substantive*. Unlike the "bad faith" approaches mentioned earlier, the beliefs held by other people should be taken as meaning exactly what they say, strange though that may be to us. Similarly, to view people of another tradition as mainly driven by anxiety, violence, hysteria, or other extra-religious reasons is simply to say that we do not regard them as religious at all. It is no threat that other faiths have a sense of sacredness or holiness that seems alien to us. Instead, such claims make it clear that some religious views simply resist comparison or connection with our own. S. Mark Heim (see Suggested Readings) has noted how our best efforts at accord still stumble over incompatible concerns, especially about the ends or "salvations" sought by different traditions. Religious difference is an irreconcilable possibility to be assessed by looking at distinctive truths and irreducible values.

If religious difference is variable, embodied, oriented, and substantive, how might preaching engage it faithfully? Certain forms of inter-religious *dialogue* are suggestive about how to rethink preaching within the frame of beliefs. To be sure, we do not mean that preaching can be the same as inter-religious dialogue. Even in light of the many extant dialogical forms of preaching, we are not speaking here about a style of presentation but instead a process of engagement in which preaching would take part. In order to understand that role more accurately, however, we must first discern the conditions for an appropriate inter-religious dialogue itself.

From the outset, such dialogue desires full *understanding*. Paradoxically, dialogue with another religion is entered into more for our own sake than for the sake of the other tradition. Christians specifically engage in dialogue out of faithfulness to the mission of Christ. That mission is, at heart, a matter of showing Christ to others rather than winning converts (which sometimes happens, too). In being understood by others as well as in understanding them better, we show the face of Christ who meets us all in mercy. This same mission-driven understanding moves us beyond defensive efforts to seek our own security. Instead, we can trust that the one who has already claimed us now guides the inter-religious encounter as well.

Closely related to this, dialogue seeks *affirmation*. Most readers would agree that we ought not aim at obliterating the distinctiveness of another religious group, but there is more at stake in this for Christians than mere tolerance. To "convert" others in this way would be a loss to everyone, for it would basically mean that an encounter with Christ (through us as the dialogue partners) is nothing other than judgment and death. Instead of this, however, we show Christ in such a way that other religions may claim more fully their own distinctive identity through an encounter with us. Christ, as source of life for the world, does not cancel out the existence of others but refines who they will be as part of the divinely ordered creation. A consistent Christian theology would include other religions within this same ambit of grace and restoration.

Dialogue also embraces a level of *risk*. Like any genuine conversation, dialogue places us into the path of potential change. This is because it is a discourse of mutual disclosure between parties rather than a mode of domineering argument or manipulation. By "mutual," we mean that the other party's perspective is honored and taken as seriously as our own. By "disclosure," we mean that we are as open and truthful with others as we would be with ourselves. We listen carefully both to grasp the alternate rationality of another tradition and to find the ways we can be most deeply heard by them.

Finally, dialogue upholds a *faithful ethics*. Foundational to the entire enterprise is an ethics of nonviolence. This is not the absence of conflict or disagreement, but a refusal to seek harm, even in speaking of other religions outside of the dialogue. Also required is an ethics of humility in which we acknowledge the ways we have, in fact, harmed other religious groups. Being self-conscious about this is both a sobering reminder to ourselves and a helpful caution to others of the violence inherent in our tradition. Building upon nonviolence and humility is an ethics of honesty. We are obliged to affirm our own perspective fully, for this is what actually makes us a valuable dialogue partner in the first place. Moreover, being intentional about this protects us from the self-deception that we are somehow objective and neutral in the dialogue. Honesty also means openly stating places of genuine difference with another tradition and even, in love, naming points of that tradition we feel bound to critique.

We have contended that the frame of beliefs must be seen in terms of genuine religious difference for which the proper response is serious inter-religious dialogue. Without this perspective, preaching is sure to founder on the rocks of assimilation (all other beliefs are the same) or denigration (no other beliefs can matter). On the other hand, when preaching is seen as part of a larger and robust dialogue with difference, it is far more capable of addressing the cross-cultural challenge of beliefs. We turn again to our interviewees to hear how religious beliefs affect preaching in the places they serve.

Group Characteristics

At this point, you may question whether there really are any significantly diverse beliefs in your place of ministry. Genuine religious difference as we have described it may seem rather remote, as does the need or even occasion for preaching to be a catalyst for inter-religious dialogue. There is good reason for this perception.

Since beliefs are highly treasured cultural expressions that address matters of ultimate significance, they are not always easily shared or readily apparent. Many beliefs are closely guarded, masked from scrutiny by others or subtly embedded in the course of daily life. Our purpose in this section, therefore, is to pass along how our interviewees began to notice that differences in beliefs were indeed significant in ways that had an effect upon their preaching. These interviews prompted us to present the group characteristics of this frame as answers to two questions. First, where do beliefs make an evident impact upon groups at an everyday level? Several remarks from our informants will suggest a range of ordinary instances to notice. Second, what do such evident, everyday beliefs imply about the kinds of difference that preaching must address in order to sponsor true dialogue? A continuum will clarify this, ranging from difficult barriers at the one end to welcome openings at the other.

Ordinary Instances

When our respondents mentioned the different kinds of beliefs they encountered, they rarely spoke of them as abstract ideas. Instead, they noted instances woven into the fabric of everyday activity. In the end, their comments clustered into four areas of daily life where religious matters seemed most evident. We present these in order of scope, from broadest to narrowest.

Although the area of *worldview* may appear speculative and removed from ordinary life, those we interviewed remarked that simple human practices sometimes conveyed a compressed sense of how reality itself is ordered and valued. When this general level of religious categorization can be discerned, however, it often has great bearing upon other portions of daily existence and what those believers understand or accept. For example, the pastor of a largely Native Alaskan congregation told us of a fishing trip with several members. They began to call to the fish they were netting, coaxing the fish to hand over their lives as food. The worldview of these members was strongly shaped by traditional Iñupiat beliefs about the pervasiveness of spirit in every part of creation, a worldview with obvious implications for congregational life and weekly preaching.

In a similar way, a preacher familiar with the Mexican immigrants in his congregation pointed out two aspects of daily life that reflected an older, pre-Christian worldview. First, he noted, "they have the four cardinal directions, the four elements of the earth, the four seasons; and even the corn, which is sacred food, has four colors." Beyond this, a traditional emphasis on fertility meant that mothers were socially significant, honored as the center of life in both home and community. These two ordinary and overlapping features—the number four and the role of the mother—dramatically affected how classic Roman Catholic doctrines were adopted, particularly in how the Trinity was seen to be "completed" through the highly venerated figure of Mary.

Of course, a religious worldview may also be evident in more direct ways rather than indirectly revealed through particular practices. A pastor whose congregation consisted of many Vietnamese immigrants noted how a generally Buddhist perspective affected the way that both daily life and specific Christian concepts were understood.

> Another concept with the Vietnamese, because most of them were associated with Buddhism, is the wheel. In Buddhism there is a wheel that stands for the wheel of life and death. And the motivation of the Buddhist is to be free from life and death, incarnation and suffering. They just want to get out from that wheel of sufferings, because they consider that life is a natural place of suffering. So in order to get away from this you have to understand the cause of suffering and do away with it, and then do good or not create any more suffering for others, or else the suffering might come back to your own children or grandchildren. And this is why Buddha is important, as a concept of enlightenment, of knowing yourself, of knowing your roots so you can get out from darkness and get into a place of light.

Recognizing this Buddhist worldview clarified for this pastor several specific matters about his members, ranging from their child-rearing practices to their disinterest in stereotypical Christian portrayals of heaven.

A second area of daily life where religious differences were noticeable was in *relationships*. In the discussion of worldview, we saw that beliefs are exposed in the comprehensive ways that reality is symbolized or life-and-death questions are addressed. By contrast, relationships expose beliefs in a more restricted sphere of social encounters, with religious views displayed in the ways other people are valued or treated. The preachers we met referred to community life, social status, moral behavior, and family concerns as instances where distinctive beliefs could be seen to exert an influence.

A Korean pastor who has served in both African American and Chinese congregations spoke of the significant way Confucian perspectives were embedded in various social institutions ranging from community to school to household.

> For Japanese, Chinese, and Koreans, a hermeneutical point that is absolutely fundamental is this Confucian residue. To make a little oversimplified point, the American ethos is individualistic and utilitarian. But in any Asian community, there's a communitarian ethos at work. You know, like you'll see a bumper sticker that says, "Question Authority!" But the Confucian principle is to trust in a very ordered and systematic way. And in Confucian values, the teacher was the most revered person in the culture. This authority given to teachers also extends to ministers and pastors. Again, one of the primary Confucian values is filial piety, respect in the treatment of elders. I would say for Asian Americans, it is much more difficult to put your aging mother or grandfather in a rest home or something. There is a kind of overwhelming commitment to the importance of the family.

While one might focus on the ethnic aspects of these comments, it is the pattern of beliefs that is especially significant for our purposes here. Across widely different Asian ethnic groups, a foundational set of religious commitments influences the basic social relations of community and home.

Throughout our research, in fact, those we interviewed often mentioned how family life in particular showed a great deal about religious commitments. The significance of Buddhist or Shinto influences was readily detected in the honor given to elders and the ritual veneration accorded to ancestors. In a very different religious system, a distinctively Roman Catholic emphasis on the Holy Family was displayed in the everyday honor and respect shown to parents in many Latino homes. Because the family is a basic training ground for both worldview (making sense of reality) and relationships (social roles and interactions), it is naturally a potent site in which beliefs will come to the fore.

Another part of daily life that is fraught with religious significance has to do with *changes* faced by individuals or groups. Whether during crisis times, rapid transformation, or slower-paced but important life passages, people are more likely to call directly upon the resources of a belief system in order to interpret the changes at hand. This corresponds to what we have already noted about how religion bears a worldview and orders relationships, both of which help negotiate a return from disorientation to some kind of normalcy.

At a group level, those we interviewed remarked that times of persecution for various ethnic or immigrant groups often had strong religious overtones. Of course, in many cases the very cause of persecution itself might have had religious roots. Beyond this, however, its ongoing significance for group identity was frequently given a religious interpretation. To explore the experiences of oppression or harm suffered by an ethnic group naturally will surface strong beliefs and faith convictions as well. For similar reasons, potent religious symbols or festivals come to be associated with the journeys and travails of a group, a matter illustrated by the frequent linkage between Roman Catholic saints and particular immigrant communities. Since the saint has been a protector during past trials, it becomes a focal point for prayer and hope in subsequent crisis times as well.

At an individual level, passages through adolescence, into marriage, or at the point of death also represent key changes where serious religious work is expended. Our respondents were quick to note that rituals during such passages were typical occasions when religious variety and difference were evident, requiring special pastoral sensitivity. One preacher recalled the funeral for a man who, in joining her congregation years earlier, had left behind his wife's religious tradition.

> We just had the funeral for a member a few weeks ago that was important because his wife was not a member. In the fifteen years he had been a member of this congregation,

his wife had never set foot in our church. She thought we had taken her husband away, that we were noisy, and I don't know what all. She wanted the funeral with her religious group and not ours, which kind of annoyed people here. Well, finally she invited us to do one of the evening services at the funeral home, and it had a tremendous impact on her. The first time she experienced us as a worshiping community was at the funeral home, and it just opened her eyes. She was very touched and moved by the experience. She had no idea what he had done in the church and she had no idea that people cared so much for him.

Such difficult occasions can inflame old religious wounds and stir potent differences in beliefs that remain dormant in more settled times. On the other hand, they also provide profound opportunities for religious understanding provided that these wounds and differences are noticed and honored.

The narrowest aspect of daily life where religious matters become evident is in the *body* itself. Piety and beliefs are ordinarily expressed in thoroughly material ways, and the body is perhaps the one material resource over which we have greatest control. Bodily practices therefore become powerful ways of symbolizing religious commitments through forms such as posture, movement, and interaction with physical surroundings.

One of our interviewees commented on the way that several ethnic groups he knew displayed a Buddhist view of reverence in their arrangements for and actions at gatherings.

The custom when they come together is that they sit flat on the floor. They leave their shoes outside to show respect. They are in the atmosphere of reverence so they might better receive the message. I've seen it in halls, temples, pagodas, and even homes: when they come, they sit on the floor and leave their shoes outside. It is like they are sitting at the feet of the creator, of the Buddha or whatever.

What is important to notice is that seemingly insignificant items like seating or shoes can point to important religious commitments. We heard comparable examples of widely differing prayer forms, ranging from relative stillness to extreme physical activity, each showing something distinctive about the participant's beliefs. Similarly, choices about attire (clothing for particular occasions), food and drink (items consumed or avoided), and physical space (arrangement into zones or proximity between people) all can become laden with religious value. Through such means, participation in a larger mystery or sacred meaning may well be signified.

Naturally, beliefs can be manifested in many other areas besides worldview, relationships, changes, and the body. People do speak directly about their beliefs, and many religious forms are plain for all to see. The four areas mentioned above are simply places in daily life where religious difference is often quite evident if one is disposed to be attentive. Beyond noticing such differences, however, we must inquire further into how they affect the possibility for dialogue with Christian beliefs and practices. In reviewing our interviews on this matter, it became clear that these differences fell along a continuum ranging from those that were sources of resistance (barriers to overcome in dialogue) to those that were reasons for encouragement (openings to pursue in dialogue). In the next two sections, therefore, we address each end of this continuum to show other group characteristics important to this frame.

Difficult Barriers

The foregoing discussion has already hinted at a significant challenge that characterizes the frame of beliefs. Religious groups often hold views or recall experiences that can, under the right circumstances, become barriers to understanding the beliefs of others. Rarely are these barriers intentionally divisive, and few if any groups are ever exempt from them, including Christians. The failure of preachers to recognize and address these blind spots, however, can foreclose on the chance for genuine dialogue, let alone cross-cultural preaching based on such a premise. Our aim in this section is to reflect what our interviewees said about religious differences that become difficult barriers, with special attention to the sources of this challenge.

One source of these barriers is that, from the perspective of a given group, particular beliefs of others are simply *alien*. The treasured religious concepts of one group may have no correlate within another group, or may represent items of little or no value amid an alternate set of religious practices. A pastor with considerable awareness of traditional Native American beliefs used the example of the absence of a Western concept of original sin among the Lakota. The classical substitutionary theory of atonement in which Jesus is sacrificed to repay the debt for sin and cleanse the stain of human evil simply has no way of taking root in such a context.

At other times, the values that remain foreign are less directly religious but still have important implications for whether different groups interact. The rural community where one of our respondents served had recently been surprised by an influx of Orthodox Jews who purchased a local processing plant and converted it for kosher production. At this pastor's prompting, his congregation planned an event to welcome and incorporate the newcomers from this distinctive religious tradition, but which met with an unexpected response.

> There had been a circus in town the previous fall. I noticed that the entire community was at the circus. We all came together to watch the elephants and lion tamers and trapeze artists do their stuff. It caused me to ask the question: What else can we all come together around? My answer was gratitude. Thus we began to work on a service of thanksgiving. Well, it soon became clear that the Orthodox Jews were not

interested. I came to see that a value we saw as particularly important was not always so for everyone. The value that we should all be able to transcend our differences was not in the Jewish community's list of highly held or cherished beliefs. Maybe years of persecution or oppression tends to diminish that value in favor of closely guarding the boundaries and setting rather rigid limits.

It is important to notice the religious dimensions of this incident. Rudeness or indifference were not involved. Instead, preserving religious boundaries and distinctions was so central to the Orthodox Jews in this situation that the congregation's effort to overcome difference made little if any sense.

Another source of barriers to understanding and dialogue is that the religious ideas and ways of others can seem *offensive*. Religions naturally point to the most sacred, ultimate, and transcendent dimensions of reality that are, for that very reason, beyond the limits of human expression. To carry out this work often requires using language and symbols that push the boundaries of meaning to the breaking point. We can easily forget that our most treasured images or terms may sound quite strange to others and even directly collide with their equally treasured beliefs.

This is easily demonstrated simply by dwelling on basic metaphors employed in a religious tradition. Most Christians are familiar, for example, with the language of being washed clean in the blood of the Lamb (see Revelation 7:14). One of our interviewees, however, told how troubling this can sound to Buddhist listeners and those influenced by those beliefs.

> Another point is the killing of animals. When we say Christ's blood was shed to save us, that's a very strong point that stops non-Christians here, because most of them are Buddhist. One of their commandments, after honoring parents, is not to kill any life form. So when we mention about Christ's blood and so forth, they say, "Hey, how can you stand for killing a lamb, killing a sheep just in order to save your own life? Are you that selfish? A sheep is also alive!" So the picture of killing a lamb or a sheep to wash your own sins is a selfish concept, thinking only of your own life.

This same pastor later remarked about similar difficulties in communion practice, where the drinking of wine stands at odds with a Buddhist prohibition against consumption of alcohol. Our interviews exposed many instances where the most seemingly innocent belief became an unintended source of discomfort or estrangement for those from a different religious group.

A third reason that barriers to understanding develop is due to a history of *friction* between religious groups. As we learned from the pastor who tried to welcome Orthodox Jews to his town, past harm produces enduring suspicion. In addition, the history of dispute between groups may be quite lengthy, originating long before any present inter-religious contact. One preacher speculated with us about how differently Muslims and Christians might relate today had a remote strand of tritheistic Byzantine Christianity not persecuted the inhabitants of the Arabian peninsula fourteen centuries ago! When such initial harm is then amplified over the years by religiously justified imperial conquest on both sides, the hope for respectful engagement with others indeed becomes faint.

One of the most powerful places to see such friction is between relatively close cousins within a broader faith tradition. Of all the hostile relations described to us, the most virulent existed between differing groups of Christians. In the case of Chinese immigrants, for example, an interviewee reported with dismay about tensions between Protestants and Roman Catholics in his community. These tensions began, of course, in disputes far removed from either China or the new home of these immigrants, but once they entered the fray, it served the purpose of distinguishing true from false believers. When identity comes under assault, as with many ethnic, class, or immigrant groups, there is a perverse logic in attacking what is familiar in order to bolster the boundaries and strength of one's own beliefs.

One final barrier to dialogue develops from the *association* of particular beliefs with a larger, nonreligious cultural agenda. While this can also be quite closely connected with the history of friction between religious groups, the further complication comes in the overidentification of a belief system with potent political, economic, or social forces. Even a casual review of Western media coverage of Islam, for example, will quickly remind us of the many times that being Muslim is blurred together with being an Arab as well as a terrorist.

Of course, the link between Christianity and American cultural hegemony is no less disturbing and, for people of other faiths, often holds at least a grain of truth. One respondent asserted that the rejection of Christianity by some Native Americans and their subsequent return to traditional beliefs could be interpreted as a refusal to accept that faithfulness equals whiteness. She went on to say:

> I'm always conscious that the church has a reputation with Indian people. Historically, the church has not always been the bearer of good news. It's been part of the oppressor. I think that has a lot to do with how the priest would walk ahead of the soldiers when they were coming to move the people out of the their land base and move them into reservations. When you look back at a history like that, there's still a segment of our community that's very distrustful of the church. They really have to listen with different ears about a church that does love them and cares about them and has good news to share with them, since the church has been oppressive through several generations.

Another pastor noted the difficulties facing Japanese immigrants who feel that "at one level they have to abandon their Japanese-ness in order to become a Christian." In a similar vein, yet another preacher said, "In terms of making the distinctions between what our Christian faith is and how we express it, I just have to say openly, 'To be Christian doesn't mean to be American!'" When the forces entangling a faith tradition with other interests have been long-standing and substantial, however, disassociating them can be an uphill struggle.

Welcome Openings

Were we to end our review of the group characteristics of this frame here, the picture would be bleak indeed. Surely the obstacles to inter-religious dialogue would be insurmountable and the chances that preaching might reach those of other beliefs would be slim. There is, however, another side to the story that emerged during our interviews, one that gives reason for encouragement. At the other end of the continuum are religious differences that create welcome openings for us to enter. Not only do these openings lead into important areas to explore with other faith traditions, but they also can direct us toward reflection and transformation within the Christian household itself. The beliefs of others may even enrich us with perspectives and possibilities to be embraced and celebrated. Those we interviewed suggested at least three general ways they encountered such opportunities.

Some openings come through concepts or symbols that have *parallels* between different religious communities. Particular faith claims might have significant analogies in other groups or comparable meanings to be pursued. Such basic connections give a reason to set aside previous mistrust for the sake of deeper understanding. For example, one respondent claimed that the historic appeal of Christianity for the Native American members of his congregation was rooted in just such a connection.

> The spiritual values go way back in their culture. There's a concept of the spirit world, and one of the reasons the gospel was so well received among these people is that they had this concept of a spirit world as a scary and evil place, and they were so pleased to hear the message that there was a force of good, too.

Another preacher noted great similarities between Buddhist and Christian views of personal transformation and religious conversion. Once recognized, such similarities made it possible in his setting to have further conversations about ethical responsibility and behavior in the community.

Particularly intriguing were those times when a strong image or other aesthetic element provided a place of contact between religious groups. The image itself might be distinctive to only one group but suggest a parallel significance for other faiths as well. A pastor in a Vietnamese setting shaped by Confucian and Buddhist views remarked about the importance of the lotus flower as providing just such a parallel.

The Vietnamese have a lot of lotus flowers in their ponds and rivers. It's a beautiful flower, clean, but comes up from dirty mud. The other religions use that as a symbol of how you get out from darkness and move up to become a beautiful blossom, ready for the light of Buddha or whatever. And Christians took that story to explain about God's grace, of how you will one day overcome Satan.

In a related way, we were often told of religious sayings that, once examined, had resonance for other groups, or even entire narratives that had analogues in several faith traditions.

As encouraging as this all seems, it is important to add that those we interviewed were cautious about parallel concepts and symbols. While every analogy declares an "is" that suggests similarity, it also asserts an equally important "is not" that preserves distinctiveness. Indeed, many persistent disputes within Christianity itself derive precisely from how the very same concept or symbol is interpreted differently. Finding a parallel with other belief systems is not an end and at times may be a dubious beginning. Our respondents emphasized that other faith traditions resist letting their treasured expressions be claimed by others and "colonized" for the sake of generic commonality, let alone subverted for the sake of religious conversion. At their best, the parallels about which we heard were used to establish trust and normalize distant or strained relations. In the longer run, they also became a basis in preaching for honesty about religious differences, a point to which we will later return.

Other sorts of welcome openings were available through religious *practices* that were mutually enriching. Certainly, the practices of differing faith communities sometimes have tremendous similarities, either in the actions taken or their underlying meanings, and thus these would seem to be further examples of the parallels we discussed above. An urban pastor we met whose congregation incorporates immigrants from across the globe mentioned one such practice.

Another "for instance" is that the Cambodian people here were predominantly Buddhist, and the use of candles and incense is really important in their kind of Buddhism. But we also have many people from Eritrea who were Orthodox in background, and again, there's candles and incense. So by using incense and candles at certain times during the church seasons, it's really important in helping them identify with their own tradition and home.

Note, however, that the actual purpose of this practice was not so much a place of connection between different believers as it was a way that each group preserved a distinctive heritage. It is this use of practices to attain alternative religious ends (again, see S. Mark Heim's work in Suggested Readings) that we wish to distinguish here.

In fact, many of the practices described to us had few if any parallels between groups, and even then of only the most strained sort. Sometimes, what made a practice helpful was that it showed something distinctive about another religious group while simultaneously prompting a further examination of one's own beliefs. For example, we heard how the decorating of graves common to several East Asian religions both clarified the veneration of ancestors in those traditions and led Christians to consider similar concerns about death in the family.

At other times, however, a practice distinctive to one group comes to be seen as a useful skill or method by those who actually hold quite different beliefs. The profound influence of Eastern meditation techniques upon many Christians is one instance of this, while the widespread adoption of martial arts exercises (which typically have deep religious roots) is another. One pastor also noted the use of traditional Native American religious practices by lifelong Christians in a mixed Anglo and Native congregation.

> Many of our folks have been members of the congregation for several generations. But now we are experiencing a rapid growth of sun dances coming back into tribal homelands, sweat lodge ceremonies, religious ceremonies that were once allegedly told to go underground in order to survive. So in our pews on Sunday we might have some traditional practitioners worshiping with us. And there are those who will consider themselves Christian and will also be practicing some of these ceremonies which help to enrich their prayer life.

This adaptation of religious practices to enhance one's own tradition was one of the most potent ways we heard for creating new openings for inter-religious dialogue.

It is significant that almost all of the practices reported by our respondents involved worship and prayer. Regardless of the faith tradition, such practices often employ fluid or even ambiguous symbols that are easily borrowed and transformed for other religious purposes. This borrowing can also renew one's own religious practices, restoring an energy and authenticity when home-grown rituals have become stale. Even so, our interviewees offered two cautionary remarks. Adapting the practices of another tradition may, to those from that group, feel more like a distortion or violation, and thus create new barriers to understanding. Incidental to our research, we met a rabbi who was quite disturbed by a local church that held an annual "Christian seder," something he viewed as a sort of religious tourism. A Native American pastor we interviewed also despaired at what he stingingly called the "Navahomogenization" by whites of distinctive rituals, as if all Native Americans embraced a monolithic religious tradition.

In addition to this concern for those from whom practices are borrowed, we were also cautioned that such borrowing can create misunderstanding within one's own household of faith. One pastor recalled an occasion when a denominational official stormed out of a prayer service that incorporated the Lakota ritual of burning sweetgrass, a practice he deemed as nothing less than pagan. In such cases, this pastor argued, a careful reconsideration of St. Paul's concern for the faith of others within the community (see 1 Corinthians 8 and Romans 14) would be well-advised.

Intentional *reflection* was a third way we heard that religious differences could open into further dialogue. Earlier in this chapter, negative histories of friction with other faiths or association with other cultural forces were named as difficult barriers. Insofar as a faith community willingly reflected upon these histories, however, new opportunities for inter-religious understanding could emerge. Beyond these more difficult cases, our interviewees recalled other instances where encountering the beliefs of others produced an "aha!" moment of self-reflective surprise. Such surprise led first to rethinking the relative values of what seemed central or peripheral in one's own beliefs, and then to appreciating other traditions in new and unexpected ways.

One such value that several respondents had begun to reconsider was the classic fear of syncretism embedded in much of Eurocentric Christianity. From this perspective, the orthodox faith risks contamination or even error if combined with other religions. The fact that respected Christians of other stripes readily add or layer Christianity with aspects of other beliefs has started to call this thinking into question. For example, some Native traditional beliefs see the world as a multiple reality in which different faiths bring complementary gifts, even as they stand in irresolvable tension. Learning this led one interviewee into a deeper appreciation for the manifold ways Christ's life was truly abundant—a far cry from blending or distorting Christianity. This reflective insight also caused a rethinking of whether syncretism is, at times, actually an accusation borne of faithlessness and fear.

Another reflective insight we heard through our research concerned the nature of religion itself. One pastor serving in a Japanese and Anglo congregation pointed out a bit of history on the subject.

> In Japan and even in China, there is a very different way of approaching religion— what we call religion. In fact, the word "religion" in Japanese didn't even exist until the mid-nineteenth century. It was a result of exposure to the West. Interestingly, the Japanese government takes a census periodically, and they also deal with religious issues. When you calculate those who say they are Shinto and those who say they are Buddhist and what not, the figure far exceeds the Japanese population by two or three times. In other words, what that means is that they are identifying themselves as both. They look at participation in religious festivals, rites, and so forth much looser.

Indeed, the notion of separate religious identities emerged for purposes of study and classification. On their own terms, many religions make no distinction between what is believed and how one lives. This very insight, prompted by an encounter with other religions, can call us back to the material aspects of our own beliefs rather than abstracting them into a system of ideas to be analyzed. Beyond this, it can lead us to seek once more the deep wisdom so necessary to the practices of Christian faith and life.

In a related way, inter-religious encounters can awaken us to suppressed elements in our own tradition. A pastor whose congregation embraces forty different nationalities commented on a small Muslim subgroup in that setting, all relatives of church members. Through them, he started to hear the allegory about the descendants of Abraham in Galatians 4 (his appointed preaching text) in a new way. "It really hit me," he told us, "that I'm speaking to folks who are descendants of Ishmael, who see that as a positive thing." From this one encounter, he started to examine other portions of scripture for their neglected elements and meanings, not only in relation to Islam but for the benefit of his entire congregation as well.

We first described the group characteristics of the frame of beliefs in terms of the many ordinary places that religious difference can be noticed. Building on this, we have now shown that these differences suggest a spectrum of barriers to and openings for further dialogue. The pressing issue for effective cross-cultural preaching is what to do now with these insights.

Preaching Strategies

The vast scope and interpretive complexity of religious difference would seem to call for a fairly obvious cross-cultural preaching strategy. It might simply be affirmed that preachers attentive to diverse beliefs should minimize any barriers to dialogue and maximize every opening. Such a truism delivers few specifics, however, and if wrongly enacted can actually be counterproductive. Dialogue is neither a mere style to be adopted nor a final goal to be reached. Instead, it is a long-term process for engaging with those who are religiously different from us, a process in which preaching plays only a part. As such, the fundamental strategy we heard from our informants was to discern the catalytic role of the sermon within a broader dialogue. Built upon this, our interviewees developed two other strategic insights, arguing that preaching should reassess claims within the Christian household and then critically connect with those holding other beliefs.

Catalytic Role

With the other frames considered in this book, we regularly heard that strategies used outside the pulpit contributed to how the sermon itself is heard in cross-cultural settings. For example, being informed about another group or immersed in its lifeworld enhances preaching effectiveness. Of course, such strategies would enhance other roles of pastoral ministry as well and do not suggest any particularly special need for preaching. An important distinction within the frame of beliefs, by contrast, is the significance of preaching in the overall trajectory of inter-religious dialogue. While such dialogue cannot be reduced to the sermon, at the same time the sermon dare not be ignored within the dialogue. It is in this sense that we speak of the catalytic role of preaching.

Strange as it may sound, one of the first strategies in this catalytic role was accepting a *dependency* upon other forms of ministry. Sometimes this meant realizing that preaching was less well suited to certain needs within the larger dialogue. Consider when misunderstandings must be corrected. One pastor we met knew that, due to conflicts long ago between missionaries and Buddhist leaders, her Laotian immigrant members still held significant misperceptions about Christianity. Even so, she said that addressing these matters "would be something we'd do in Christian education rather than homiletical types of things, because it takes a lot more explanation than you have time for on Sunday morning." At other times, preaching must yield to forms that proclaim the gospel in more powerful ways. A Latino Lutheran pastor who sought to build bridges with Roman Catholics in his community remarked that "so much of the preaching that's appreciated and responded to here really takes place many times outside of the main liturgy—it rarely takes place on Sundays." Such comments did not reflect any despair about the place of preaching but instead showed a healthy and focused realism about what it could and could not do.

A related strategy recommended by those we interviewed was to recognize the distinctive *character* of preaching. Although these pastors cared deeply about preaching, in the end they had abandoned the heroic (and typically Protestant) idea that it is the most important pastoral task, which inevitably requires the pulpit to bear a weight it cannot support. Interestingly, this more modest view of preaching led them to focus on its unique capacities for religious dialogue. Even when the sermon form was a monologue, for example, they employed devices that activated dialogue within the minds of their listeners (use of stories, conversational style, posing questions, and so forth). By initiating this kind of internal dialogue about religious matters, the sermon therefore gave permission to notice and understand the beliefs of others. In so doing, it also modeled a process of engagement that was consistent with the larger purpose of inter-religious dialogue.

Of course, preaching is not an innocent participant in the process of dialogue. Our respondents spoke of the *potency* of preaching as an important strategic consideration in engaging the beliefs of others. Since preaching is an authoritative and intentional faith declaration, it can powerfully shape any larger inter-religious dialogue of which it is a part. Able to initiate, sustain, and direct such a conversation, preaching can also inadvertently distort or derail its development. This not only calls for greater clarity and caution about what is preached, but also a good bit of patience about the outcome. A preacher who served congregations where traditional Native beliefs were a lively force related the lengthy process by which a conversation about beliefs finally arose.

> After a few years there I got to know a lot of the leaders quite well. One, who was a very good friend, was one of the real leaders there. It was not until after I'd known him for probably four years—after that length of time, of trust level—that he began to tell me about the Native spirituality that was still a part of their lives. They were blending this stuff together and had been all along, and as clergy we were either oblivious to it or simply did not want to hear it. It took that long for him to trust me so that he could talk to be about these issues.

Only later did this pastor learn how his preaching led to deeper dialogue by giving an authoritative signal that understanding was possible. This power dynamic therefore poses a strategic challenge. Effective cross-cultural preaching must clearly authorize that engagement with other beliefs is desired while at the same time intentionally declare one's own convictions.

Our respondents also had reflected on the *principles* that guide their preaching to be attentive to other beliefs. As the incident above amply demonstrates, we may be quite unaware that our preaching already indicates to those of other beliefs the kind of dialogue partner we would likely become. For this reason, one suggestion was to review our preaching for its honesty about our own religious group (strengths, commitments, blind spots, faults) and its fairness about others (knowledge, sensitivity, invisibility, caricature). Sermons also show our principles in another way, of course, by directly naming the rationale for further dialogue itself. In this case, the intent is more to reach those within the household than those of another tradition. In the midst of trying to promote dialogue between Christians and Jews in his community, one preacher spoke of how his motivating principles had significantly changed.

> I used to speak about tolerance in sermons. I guess that now I find it better to reflect on the surprising creativity that God still speaks into the world. The Hasidim here have brought an interesting if at times perplexing diversity to a community that, left to its own resources, would never have been able to make that happen. I see all these things as the spinning out of a God whose energy creates living order in the midst of deadly chaos. I am coming to see that the important category for working in cross-cultural situations is to deepen this awareness of God's creative energy.

Note that this preacher meant to "deepen this awareness" primarily for those within the congregation. Clarifying this principle became an important strategy for cross-cultural preaching that eventually led into fuller dialogue.

Acknowledging the dependency, character, potency, and principles of cross-cultural preaching exposes its distinctively catalytic role in inter-religious dialogue. To be sure, such strategies offer only preliminary design techniques and content guidelines. More important than this, however, our interviews revealed the need for fundamental understandings out of which more specific preaching strategies can later grow. Without first taking seriously the catalytic dimension of the sermon within the frame of beliefs, other strategies easily become hollow and even manipulative, with the risk that genuine understanding would be undercut from the start.

Reassess Claims

Earlier in this chapter, we mentioned that Christians engage in dialogue with those of other religions out of faithfulness to the mission of Christ. In seeking to be understood by others, however, we inevitably enter into a self-reflective process about our own traditions. Why are certain claims essential? Which should be reconsidered? What kind of Christ are we showing to those of other beliefs? Questions like these expose that inter-religious dialogue is risky for ourselves first of all. Cross-cultural preaching embedded in such dialogue engages this risk precisely by raising these questions within the household of Christian faith. By making mention of religious differences, our respondents used their sermons to create a climate in which our own faith claims could be properly reassessed. Our interviews revealed at least three ways this can happen in preaching.

First of all, the pastors we met tried through their preaching to clarify what was religiously *acceptable* for faithful Christians. We have already noted how the beliefs and practices of one group can seem peculiar or even dangerous to another. Our respondents recognized that often their primary preaching task was to disentangle the unfamiliarity of another religious group from the hasty conclusion that its words and deeds were therefore wrong. In many cases, a simple explanation in a sermon was all it took. A Vietnamese pastor learned that some of his members viewed the Buddhists in their neighborhood as holding a crude form of idolatry. When he pursued this, he learned that these members had interpreted an ethnic posture for asking questions or seeking help as a religious posture of worship and adoration. The pastor clarified this in a sermon, which opened up new questions and subsequent sermon responses, and eventually led to a meeting with those from the local Buddhist community.

Not all barriers are so easily set aside. Sometimes the unfamiliar ways of others can be used in sermons to probe what is essential to Christian practices. In a diverse multi-ethnic setting, Buddhist rituals concerning ancestors became a point of confusion for local Christians. The pastor we interviewed went beneath the surface level of these rituals to speak with his congregation about the core human significance of remembrance. Referring to Old Testament and even modern Jewish perspectives, he helped his congregants reclaim what was essential about remembrance within their own tradition without ignoring the differences between themselves and their Buddhist neighbors. In another case, funeral traditions in a largely Puerto Rican immigrant area had led to tensions. In particular, the custom among Roman Catholics of saying the rosary on the nine evenings following a funeral had become a flash point of controversy with Protestants. The Protestant pastor we met simply asked in a sermon why this custom would be meaningful to Roman Catholics in the first place. When the members of her congregation began to see the serious need to show honor and devotion during such times of pain and loss, they could also appreciate the depth of what was at stake for Roman Catholics. Moreover, they began to explore for themselves what might be the correlate practices of reverent respect in their own congregation.

Explanation and focus on essentials may even lead to a further level of acceptance in which the religious insights of others may be adopted by Christians as well, at least with certain adaptations. A common example that we heard from respondents with Native American neighbors and congregants was the vision quest motif familiar to several tribal traditions. A pastor told us about a recent sermon that focused on this.

> Particularly at the age of the onset of puberty, it was common to send a young man out into the wilderness for some extended prayer time. It would be a time of prayer and fasting. It would be a time where this person would be alone. In many of these instances, it would be up on a hill, a high hill where one might be able to sit and see out quite a ways. The idea of it was that, even though this was an individual activity, it was really an activity of the community because the community wanted that person to go out on the hill to find one's vision, to see what one is called to do in life. As we looked at the biblical text a couple of Sundays ago about Jesus' wilderness experience, his going out into the desert for forty days and forty nights, he basically also was coming into his own understanding of what he was called to do.

The pastor then described how she had been guided in the traditional format of a vision quest herself, both to clarify her calling and to be strengthened by the Native community. Validated by the story of Jesus' testing and the pastor's own example, it became possible to explore the vision quest as a model for deeper journeys of Christian spiritual reflection as well. Other respondents told of comparable instances in which East Asian spiritual exercises were explained and affirmed in sermons. The point here is not the wholesale adoption of alternative religious practices but instead a clarification of what is acceptable in light of core Christian commitments.

A second strategy for reassessing claims in cross-cultural preaching was to let the questions and observations of other traditions reawaken what Christians have *neglected*. Earlier, we mentioned parallel concepts or symbols as points of contact between different religious groups. These parallels were used by some of our respondents to illumine somewhat diminished or overlooked aspects of Christianity. In a congregation rich with multiple ethnic and religious backgrounds, one preacher gave a lengthy example that initially seems anything but parallel.

> There is a story of the demigod Maui, which is both Hawaiian and found throughout the Polynesian world, that illustrates how the islands were formed. He and his brothers went out to go fishing. He dove down to the bottom of the ocean with part of the jawbone of his grandmother. He made it into a hook, then hooked it onto the bottom of the ocean, tied a line to it, and came back to the surface. He told his brothers to start rowing away from the line but not to look back—whatever they heard, they were not to look back. So they rowed, and they tugged on the line, and they heard this tremendous roar because the bottom of the ocean was coming to the surface, and they panicked. And at one point they looked back, and when they looked back the line snapped, and the land that had come to the surface was scattered and blown all around, and that became the chain of islands. And the parallel is where Jesus said that anyone who puts his hand to the plow and looks back is not worthy of the kingdom. Why is that? Because there are going to be terrifying moments in the transformation of our life to be persons more fully available to God, and it's going to cost us. And it's not so much that Jesus is saying this is a punishment as much as this is just the way it is. Once we start moving forward, we don't dare look back, because then it gets fragmented and we spend a great deal of time trying to pull the pieces together again.

In this way, a story from one belief system gave the leverage to pay closer attention to a Christian text that might otherwise have sounded obscure. Religious motifs from one tradition can also amplify Christian motifs that have perhaps been silenced over time, as another respondent noted.

> Well, take the feast day of Our Lady of Guadalupe, for example. We don't have that many Mexican Americans in this congregation, so there isn't an immediate identification with that symbol. But I still use it to invite people to look at their own heritage. You know, where is the divine feminine? What does this mean for how you believe? And there are all sorts of parallels in Laotian mythology and American Indian mythologies and European mythologies. Somewhere in our soul we know these things, and I seek just to draw that out.

While parallels are one way to surface neglected Christian beliefs, sources of inter-religious offense are another. We naturally fear that when a Christian claim affronts another tradition, all conversation must come to a halt. By contrast, several pastors we met used such breakdowns to uncover alternative Christian approaches that might be palatable for all the dialogue partners. We mentioned earlier a preacher who recognized that Lakota traditional religion had no sense of a doctrine of original sin and thus no way of embracing the classical substitutionary theory of atonement. Instead of giving up at this point, however, he searched out other ways that Christians have conveyed the saving work of Christ. The Eastern Orthodox view of salvation as healing ended up having great resonance with his Native American congregants. In another case, the scandal of blood atonement for Buddhists led a respondent to emphasize in his Lenten preaching the "happy exchange" (human guilt exchanged for divine righteousness) instead of more sacrificial views of the crucifixion.

The examples above bring us to a final strategy for reassessing the claims of Christianity. Careful listening to other religious groups and thoughtful study of the breadth and depth of Christianity led many respondents to focus in sermons on the *multiplicity* of Christian traditions. When offense was caused especially by reducing of Christianity to one (usually ethnic) form, the needed remedy was to reclaim other ways to be faithful as a Christian. Instead of producing some sort of theological relativism, the result was an affirmation that the wide channel of Christianity can be navigated by different vessels along varying routes. In one case, a pastor called upon members from four diverse Christian traditions to enact portions of the Good Friday texts as the sermon for the day. The jarring religious visions that emerged were a powerful proclamation of how the crucifixion has many meanings, all equally faithful. At other times, remembering Christian multiplicity creates an internal critique. By referring to the treasure of dance among Roman Catholic Latinos, one interviewee was then able to confront the historic prohibition of dance among Native Alaskan Protestants. What is interesting in these examples and others is the way that the sermon, as part of a larger dialogue, leads to change *within* the Christian household. When we reassess claims by looking for the acceptable, the neglected, and the multiple in our own tradition, then we become the ones who are renewed by the encounter with other beliefs.

Critically Connect

Our respondents never assumed that accurately understanding the beliefs of others or honestly reassessing our own claims diminished the distinctiveness of Christianity. In fact, giving a faithful Christian witness in inter-religious dialogue demands a clear statement of our own religious perspective. Without this, we not only fail to be true to our deepest convictions but also cease to be a serious conversation partner for others. Preaching that contributes to such dialogue seeks to connect with other religions, but always critically. To act "critically," however, means something other than the typical caricature of negativity and fault-finding. Instead, being critical is really a matter of wise and patient discernment. At the right time and in the right way, effective cross-cultural preachers discover how to tell the truth in dialogue with other beliefs. They know their own traditions and can calmly, nondefensively declare what links can and cannot be made with other traditions. Those we interviewed named three ways they worked toward this in their sermons.

As an initial strategy, we were told of the need to be *responsible* within preaching in an inter-religious setting. This partly meant acknowledging the harm done to the dialogue partner in the past through insensitivity, caricature, friction, or negative associations. Neither the scale of the harm nor the actual presence of those from the other tradition were as important as simply using the potent occasion of the sermon to signal fault and repentance. Beyond this, being responsible meant declaring in and for the congregation what would guide its inter-religious engagement in the future. That is, we learned that honesty in dialogue demands basic clarity within one's own group about what will motivate and constrain the encounter. A Lutheran pastor we met told of two such guidelines that he had mentioned in a sermon to indicate to his congregation why a dialogue should proceed.

> The first comes from Luther's explanation of the commandment not to bear false witness. He said this means we are to defend our neighbors, speak well of them, and put the best construction on everything. It is easy to turn differences into wrong, evil, foolish behavior. It is healthier to see how you can put others in the best light possible. Another thing that is useful to remember is that we are most often surprised by grace as it comes to us through the stranger or through thought patterns or cultural ways that are not our own.

A wise interaction with and even differentiation from another tradition cannot occur without a prior agreement on the rules for that engagement. Preaching can operate responsibly in a larger dialogue, therefore, by enunciating both a penitent and a principled beginning.

Earlier in this chapter, we noted that some practices and aesthetic elements created welcome openings between different religions by highlighting complementary parallels. At that same point, we also said that the "is" of every such connection was accompanied by an equally important "is not" of difference. Those earlier comments set the stage here for a second preaching strategy for critical connecting, that of using such practices and aesthetic elements in order to *clarify* one's own tradition to others. Recall that our informants were vocally opposed to casually appropriating and distorting the treasures of another religious tradition. Even so, because these treasures are often symbolically rich and multivalent, they naturally can bear many alternative meanings. Recognizing this, preachers sometimes explored these different meanings with care and dignity in order to differentiate two traditions.

Among Christian groups, a strong symbol might be held completely in common and yet also be used in preaching to illumine key differences. A pastor we interviewed served a Protestant congregation in an overwhelmingly Roman

Catholic area where serious religious tensions had developed between the two groups. She knew that although there was no real disagreement in baptismal theology between the two traditions, there were many differences in piety. As a result, she explored in a sermon several distinctive Catholic practices surrounding baptismal water, such as vessels for holy water or rites of sprinkling. Instead of driving the two groups further apart, her honesty about the different pieties actually created the ground for mutual respect and opened the way for closer bonds between the groups.

In cases of much wider inter-religious difference, the sermonic strategy obviously needs to be rather different. When one group employs a practice that has no parallel in another, the deeper meaning of the practice may instead become the point of critical contact in preaching. An informant spoke of a Thai practice of tying strings around the wrist to mark when an infant becomes three months old or to remember and honor an ancestor. This minister learned that the practice had religious significance in expressing both celebration and thanksgiving. Referring to this religious significance in a sermon, he was then able to point out contrasting ways Christians understand and mark a similar religious impulse, but through forms like prayer, song, and the eucharistic meal. The significance and integrity of the actual practice was respected in its own right while at the same time being used to indicate the different ways and beliefs of Christians.

As a final strategy of critical connection, those we interviewed crafted sermons that gave an overt *account* of Christian beliefs within an inter-religious encounter. Out of a misplaced desire not to offend, some readers might imagine that sensitive cross-cultural preaching ought to avoid or suppress such potentially divisive topics. The strange fact, however, is that this very strategy was actually one of the most important for catalyzing genuine dialogue. In some cases, to be sure, all that was needed was simply to correct a misperception about an aspect of Christian theology or practice. At other points, however, the effort required a more elaborate yet accessible teaching about a particular doctrine. All the other strategies mentioned up to this point would clearly contribute to making such teaching accessible to those of another tradition. Even so, explaining deep religious commitments usually demanded considerable background work and study for those we interviewed. Giving an account of one's own beliefs in a full and accurate manner is at least as challenging as trying to understand the beliefs of others, if not more so.

The preachers we met regularly mentioned three areas of Christian belief for which they sought to render an account. The first was the relationship between the particularity and universality of Christ as Savior. As we noted earlier, many traditions seek religious ends that look nothing like what Christians view as salvation. At the same time, our informants said that people of other faiths wanted to know how Christians could both be thoroughly oriented to the singular figure of Jesus and yet assert that this figure holds cosmic significance. Our respondents especially focused on explaining that the universality of Christ does not entail the elimination of other beliefs and that the particularity of Christ does not entail a culturally constrained and parochial mode of believing.

Related to this, the preachers we interviewed tried to offer a special account of the religious distinctiveness of Christian incarnational theology. Attention to this subject made it abundantly clear that Christians do not view earthly existence as an unreal appearance or something to be avoided or overcome. This move drew an honest contrast not only with several Eastern religious traditions but also with the functional gnosticism pervasive in American civil religion. A robust incarnational theology emphasizes to others the view that God, through Christ Jesus, is familiar with pain and suffering and enters into the depth of human existence, utterly committed to restoring the creation to whole and abundant life.

A third area about which our interviewees made a more elaborate account in their preaching was the historically embedded nature of the Christian faith. Christianity does not depend upon a collection of timeless propositional truths or a compliance with doctrinal positions. Instead, it is rooted in a distinctive narrative of history and hope, a biblical story of God's commitment to a particular people intended toward a specific future. This distinguishes how Christians interpret sacred texts, for example, since divine revelation is not divorced from cultural forms or historical embodiment. It also distinguishes how Christians view time itself, not as a cyclical or fatalistic pattern in which all is determined, but instead as a dynamic reality through which we remember God's persistent faithfulness and anticipate God's life-giving promise.

Preaching that accounts for these sorts of theological commitments in the course of inter-religious dialogue ideally affects Christian hearers most of all. It offers them an internal critique by focusing on what is truly central in their own beliefs. Moreover, it declares a position from which they can remain appropriately open to external critique by other traditions, in order to develop a renewed and deepened witness to Christ. Finally, it reminds them that Christianity is fully embedded in cultural forms while remaining profoundly counter-cultural. Effective cross-cultural preaching shows a faith that is not rigidly bound to any one situation but is instead both grounded and adaptive, seriously engaging other religious traditions with a discerning and generous spirit.

6. Insights and a Final Voice

We began this book by saying that those who wish to take cross-cultural preaching seriously should grasp the importance of recognition. When we use that term, recognition means not only honor (respecting dignity) but also familiarity (developing appreciation) and finally insight (rethinking commitments). Although these three aspects of recognition ought to be treated inseparably, for purposes of clarity we have focused in earlier chapters mostly upon recognition as honor and familiarity. We were guided, for example, by the theological image of "neighbor" in order to *honor* those among whom we preach. Building on this, we listened closely to our interviewees in order to attain *familiarity,* frame by frame, with the situations and experiences of these same neighbors.

In this final chapter, we concentrate more directly on recognition as *insight.* Because such insight is a self-reflective activity, these closing remarks will introduce less by way of new understandings about the cross-cultural neighbor. Instead, our attention will center primarily upon *preachers* themselves and their *preaching.* Many times already, we have heard hints from interviewees of how cross-cultural challenges led to a re-examination of what it meant to be a pastor and preacher. Moreover, by being in the vanguard of those facing such challenges from the pulpit, these same persons have begun to consider how preaching itself is changing—not so much in individual sermons, but the overall task of public proclamation. Our effort is therefore to share a summary of these new insights about preachers and preaching, with special attention to several theological implications.

Insights about Preachers

During the course of our research, preachers who were not part of the project would hear about our work and express great interest in it. Almost invariably, they wanted to learn how to "read audiences" from different cultural groups in order to customize their sermons accordingly. As logical and laudable as that approach first seems, it assumes that the real challenge is outside of the preacher and can be met by developing new skills. Our respondents saw things differently, however, recommending that genuine change began with the very role of the preacher. Even though the ultimate goal is to reach out to the neighbor, effective cross-cultural preachers actually began with an inward rather than outward impulse.

Knowing Yourself

Many of our interviewees said that one of their biggest mistakes came in ignoring their own culture. They were intimately familiar with the cultures in which they were raised and still lived, but rarely did they consciously consider the assumptions on which their daily activities and interactions rested. As one person put it, "If birds were suddenly endowed with scientific curiosity, they might examine many things, but the sky itself would be overlooked as a suitable subject. If fish were to become curious about the world, it would never occur to them to begin by investigating water." Birds and fish would take sky and sea for granted, unaware of their profound influence, because they comprise the medium for every act. The cultural universe that is home to us pulls us into shared experiences with some while separating us from others. This happens so naturally and automatically that we are usually oblivious to it happening at all.

The language we first learn as children exemplifies how unaware we often are of our cultural universe. Not until we try to learn a second language do we usually begin to pay attention to the nature and rules of the language we have spoken our entire lives. In a similar way, when our interviewees began to pay attention to other cultures, it became the impetus to focus inwardly upon their own cultural universe. In this regard, one respondent wondered whether many preachers perhaps actually live in the universe of American cultural religion where the oppressive actions of certain corporations are never labeled as sin. Such actions are simply invisible, just part of the way things are. Another interviewee noted that preachers seldom ask questions like, "Why am I doing this as a white, North American, middle-aged preacher?" Challenges like these drive home the point that our own cultural universe is not culturally universal—a necessary first step toward adopting and using effective cross-cultural strategies.

Once this sort of self-reflective cultural work has been seriously undertaken, there is no turning back. One pastor used the metaphor of coming out of a box to describe the growth that followed an examination of her own culture. "I was in my own little box and I didn't even know it," she told us. "Then I was exposed to all these new things—different ways of seeing the world. You can never again fit yourself into your original, monocultural box." Another preacher affirmed his new cultural awareness by saying, "There is no way that I can go back, as rich as it was at the time. I know too much now to even want to go back to that."

Although such growth in cultural self-awareness is irreversible, it can also be profoundly liberating. A preacher serving a Latino community told of how she experienced that setting as frustrating until she spent some time examining her own Scandinavian roots. Her congregation's way of doing things was much more open and emotive than that of her own ethnic heritage. "Our council meetings are crazy," she told us. "They are very noisy. People tend to talk all at the same time." After realizing that her perceptions of "proper" communication were drawn simply from her own ethnic background, she learned she was actually quite capable of expanding her comfort range in communication. It was simply that no one had ever challenged her to explore this aspect of herself. She celebrated the change in her personality resulting from what she referred to as "yin-yang psychology." On the one hand she still had her old roots, but on the other hand her exposure to a very different culture enriched her personality and, in turn, her preaching. What is important to notice, however, is that this all began with an honest look at her own cultural starting point.

Accepting Difference

An honest inward focus also involves facing genuine differences that exist between cultures. The term *neighbor* reminds us that, although such people may be near to us, they are neither members of our household nor are we members of theirs. This can be painful. Some preachers told us they long to eliminate cultural boundaries completely and be at one with the people to whom they minister and preach. No matter how hard they try, however, personal factors such as family, history, and education make them different from those they so desperately want to reach. One preacher described this by saying, "You can't fake a culture that's not your own. You can respect it, learn from it as a visitor, but you can't ape it."

The impossibility of completely entering another culture can result in a "stranger complex." Cross-cultural preachers need to realize they will always feel somewhat like strangers amid the very people they serve. No matter how well such preachers listen, no matter how broadly they read, no matter how carefully they shape what they say, they remain outsiders. Not only does the preacher know it, but so do the culturally diverse members of the congregation. While this does not prevent the possibility of effective preaching, the stranger complex should be recognized as a persistent and unavoidable job hazard for the cross-cultural preacher.

A vivid illustration of this came during a conversation with a very self-aware preacher we met in the course of our interviews. Having grown up in the South, he already knew of his family and regional legacy of racism. As a result, he had done a considerable amount of personal reflection on these issues. Even so, he re-counted that when he came to serve a Midwestern congregation with members from a lower socioeconomic background, he was blindsided by the issue of class.

He discovered his insensitivity to how his upbringing and attitudes reflected upper-middle-class values. Once he recognized his class-bound thinking, he worked hard to understand his own reactions and how he might preach effectively in what was for him a very different culture. In spite of all his efforts, it remained an uphill struggle. Despite his sensitivity and all of his efforts, class difference would always remain a difference. Although this preacher and others told us that this gnawing frustration cannot be avoided, it still must be acknowledged.

This is not, however, a counsel of despair. Acknowledging and accepting genuine differences has theological implications. The church has always been understood as a community whose members are fundamentally different from each other. The apostle Paul describes the church using the image of the human body composed of parts as different as hands, feet, and eyes (1 Corinthians 12:12-26). In so doing, he argues for the necessity of such differences. The hand is not a foot, and we would be in trouble if it were. Moreover, this body metaphor connects our differences to Christ. If we take seriously the one we claim as Lord, we must expect and embrace differences. It is necessary for members of the church to be different in order for the church to be the body of Christ in and for the world.

Whether the stranger complex is a frustration, a challenge, or a source of celebration depends on the degree to which we embrace this vision of the nature of the church, a vision of disparate members baptized into one body (1 Corinthians 12:13). The goal has never been to homogenize the people of God but to move to a greater mutual understanding and appreciation of our differences. To dwell only on our limited ways of joining with other cultures can indeed produce despair. By contrast, to embrace the theological depth of human diversity can free us to rejoice in those differences whose unity is found in being joined together in Christ.

Facing Discomfort

Although this book presumes a respect for cultural differences (a value we suspect our readers share), such appreciation is by no means natural. In a curious twist, cultural anthropologist F. M. Keesing argues that ethnocentrism itself is a universal tendency by which a group confers upon its own people and society a central position of priority and worth. Ethnocentrism becomes the window through which each ethnic group comes to interpret and judge all others. The logical extension of such ethnocentrism is the view that "our way is the right way." It takes little imagination to see that this claim holds true not only for ethnic realities but also for the other cultural frames we have examined. We have a tendency to value only the way our class or fellow believers do things.

Despite our theological affirmations of the diversity of the creation and especially in the body of Christ, such a concept runs counter to something deep within each of us. We are children of a fallen creation, born with an instinct for survival, not altruism. Sin draws us in upon ourselves. Rejection of cultural difference is therefore something that must be unlearned. Deeper still, for Christians it requires a repentance and transformation to be worked in us by the Spirit. Even after such a change, of course, we still live in weakness and imperfection, subject to the power of sin that draws us back into the safety of our own ethnicity, class, and so forth. When we preach across cultures, therefore, we ought to expect a very real discomfort due to the persistence of this sinful, survival-oriented nature. Such discomfort is theologically important and should not be ignored, since this is what ultimately drives us again into repentance for the amendment of our lives. At the same time, however, we also want to draw attention here to another kind of discomfort that is equally important to claim. This is the discomfort that is natural to the learning process in any type of cross-cultural work.

Educators Mildred Sikkema and Agnes Niyekawa (consult the Suggested Readings) observe that learning in a cross-cultural setting takes place in four stages: (1) disorganization, (2) re-examination and reflection, (3) reorganization, and (4) emergence of new perspectives. These authors note that the first stage of *disorganization* includes "acute feelings of personal discomfort" because familiar practices and forms of interaction simply do not work. Those who intentionally attempt cross-cultural preaching will naturally face the same kind of disorganization-stage discomfort as do cross-cultural learners in other settings. When beginning to deal with a culture significantly different from their own, preachers can expect disorientation, anxiety, and frustration, because the usual ways of operating are no longer successful. Some of our interviewees referred to just such poignant feelings of discomfort. Often their first efforts at preaching and ministry did not go well, and they expressed their frustration in terms of annoyance, irritation, exasperation, and confusion. It was also common for them to experience a temporary loss of self-esteem.

These feelings are unpleasant but imperative for growth. They are part of the unlearning that needs to take place before the necessary learning can occur. Some theorists refer to this discomfort as "positive disintegration," a situation in which learners are in disharmony with both themselves and their environment. This tearing down of old ways of seeing things prepares the way for the second stage of *re-examination and reflection*. This is a time of taking stock of new, albeit potentially painful, insights. Preachers described this stage as one of becoming more aware of and open to their own cultural biases. It is a particularly important time for preachers to have the kind of support base discussed in the next section of this chapter. Re-examination and reflection went better for most preachers we interviewed when they had supportive people with whom they could process what they were learning.

While the initial stages of the Sikkema and Niyekawa schema involve a kind of dismantling of cultural perspectives, the remaining stages suggest a reconstruction. The third stage of *reorganization* is marked by the emergence of new feelings about both one's own culture and the new culture that is being encountered. We have already referred at several points in this book to preachers whose exploration of cross-cultural settings led them to claim more deeply their own backgrounds as well. Building upon such reorganization is the fourth stage of *emergence of new perspectives*. This stage is characterized by gaining a sufficient understanding of a new culture so as to appreciate both the limits and the possibilities of that knowledge. It was at this very point that preachers finally felt prepared to generalize from what they had learned in order to plan appropriate homiletical strategies.

Seeking Support

Regardless of the setting for preaching, it is intimidating to realize that the difference between success or failure often rests squarely on the preacher's own shoulders. This responsibility can seem overwhelming. The many challenges and complexities found in culturally diverse settings add further pressure. Our interviewees warned us of the considerable stress that can mount over time. They frequently stated how important it was for them to seek a solid base of support, especially with those whose cultural situation was reasonably similar to their own.

Far from being a kind of safety net or evasion of cross-cultural immersion, our respondents saw such support as crucial to genuinely effective ministry over the long run. Over many years, one pastor had observed many different Anglo preachers serve Native American congregations on reservations in his area. He argued there was a direct correlation between the level of support these preachers developed within their own cultural heritage and the longevity and effectiveness of their ministry on reservations. "Success is possible to the degree that someone has a support system off the reservation—people who are there to listen, to understand, to encourage, and to be supportive of the person, even though they might not understand that well what they are experiencing culturally. But they have an interest that's real, and they are willing to listen and be supportive of that person. That's extremely important."

Ministry models from scripture echo this advice to have a community of support, no matter how small. When Jesus sent his disciples to battle unclean spirits, he did not expect them to go alone but sent them out two by two (Mark 6:7). Each disciple had a familiar member from his group nearby for support. When the burden of leadership became too great for Moses, his own father-in-law, Jethro, instructed him to seek out qualified help (Exodus 18). During his difficult missionary journeys, Paul typically traveled with co-workers (Acts 13). The common feature here is not companionship for its own sake but the support of others as an empowerment for effective ministry.

We met preachers who sought such support both within and beyond the congregations in which they served. The key, however, was that the support came from someone native to the preacher's own background, in whatever way that background was described. Preachers who lacked such a support base in attempting to do cross-cultural ministry were urged by our respondents to be active in establishing one. Naturally, one might first turn to those who already provide love and care but with whom the stress and frustration of cross-cultural preaching has not previously been discussed. Although it is ideal to have such partners nearby for face-to-face conversation, having someone on the other end of the telephone or Internet was seen as far better than trying to work with no support base at all.

Being Flexible

As noted earlier in this chapter, our respondents advised that effective preachers cannot simply adopt the cross-cultural setting in which they serve, nor should they try. There are some important exceptions to this, however. By far the most common was the need for flexibility regarding delivery. To be sure, this was an area of great struggle for many of our interviewees. Early in their preaching ministry, many had settled on a style of delivery that was familiar because of ethnicity, prior experience, or even personality. In addition, these styles were used because they were comfortable for their hearers. The challenge came when these preachers moved to a new, culturally diverse setting or when such a setting grew up around them. The new hearers often had quite different ideas of what constituted appropriate sermon delivery.

Although their specific struggles differed greatly, these respondents agreed that cross-cultural preachers needed to be flexible enough to rethink their delivery style if it did not fit the expectations of their hearers. For some, this meant changing from preaching with a manuscript to delivering the sermon conversationally from brief notes. For others, the change was in the opposite direction, from extemporaneous to manuscript delivery. While such differences may at first seem minor, research by Albert Merrabian and others indicates that the actual communication impact may be quite significant. Taking into account all the "imaginable units of meaning" that are possible in any oral presentation, only 8 percent of the meaning for the hearer comes from the verbal content. Paralanguage (inflection, volume, and rate) comprises 37 percent of the meaning, and nonverbal or body language provides the remaining 55 percent. Since over nine-tenths of the meaning is therefore tied to matters of delivery (paralanguage and body language), the experience of a sermon can be dramatically affected by items as small as the decision to use manuscript or notes.

This does not mean, of course, that the words preachers employ are unimportant. We have already heard many times in this book that the use of scripture and the choice of examples or stories need to be appropriate to the cross-cultural situation. Nor does this imply that certain forms of sermon notation automatically produce stronger or weaker kinds of delivery. Some preachers are adept at using a manuscript in a virtually transparent fashion while others can appear stiff and distant even when using few if any notes. We are simply wanting to stress that the experiential meaning of the sermon for a hearer is greatly influenced by the delivery style, with important consequences for cross-cultural preachers to consider.

After some initial resistance, one preacher abandoned using a manuscript because he realized it was a barrier for many in his congregation. They cared less about a sophisticated and finely crafted sermon than about the genuineness with which the preacher spoke of what he believed. For his congregation, "It [the message] has got to show in your voice. It's got to show in your face. It's got to show in your gestures, in your nonverbal body language and movements—that what I'm communicating is very important, and it's from the heart." Ultimately he recognized that in this setting, he could not show all this and still use a manuscript.

On the other hand, another pastor learned a similar need for flexibility but in a very different direction. His previous experience had been in a large African American congregation where he preached extemporaneously. The members appreciated his delivery because they liked someone who preached "happy." He then served in a predominately Japanese American and Chinese American church. In an effort to be authentic and engaging, he naturally preached in his customary "happy" style. "I got happy," he told us. "I got *myself* happy, preaching in this Japanese and Chinese setting, and it just went over like a lead balloon—just nothing." In this case, he had to shift from a highly energetic and informal style to a more reserved and deliberate approach grounded in a manuscript. Both examples point to the need for keen sensitivity to the cultural expectations of specific congregations regarding delivery.

Flexibility in delivery referred to more than just the form of sermon notation. We also learned that effective cross-cultural preachers have learned to adapt to changes of direction in the midst of the sermon, regardless of where the preaching originally intended to go. For example, one preacher told us she moved to a congregation where it was typical for hearers to react aloud during the sermon. Not to adjust and incorporate this interaction into the sermon would have been offensive if not disastrous. As a result, her preaching style changed as she sought to connect with the group's responsive spirituality. She added that this has led at times to saying something totally different than she planned because her hearers responded differently than she expected.

This advice about flexibility also aims at a deeper level than simply delivery and presentation. On the one hand, we need to be honest about ourselves, accepting the inevitable influence of our own cultural universe. On the other hand, we need to step out of our comfortable cultures in order to engage the diversity of our listeners. This paradoxical flexibility, knowing ourselves while adapting to others, is ultimately a matter of trust. The effective cross-cultural preachers we met had learned to trust God to transform their gifts and efforts. The encouragement of the apostle Paul is particularly apt: "Do not be conformed to this world, but be transformed by the renewing of your minds, so that you may discern what is the will of God—what is good and acceptable and perfect" (Romans 12:2). Such transformation does not mean simplistic conformity to a role or setting, but produces instead an inversion of our values and our whole selves. It does not reduce the challenges or effort facing cross-cultural preachers, but creates instead the space in which to be truly flexible, open even to discerning God's will for our preaching.

Insights about Preaching

Our interviews with those in cross-cultural settings reveal something in addition to a renewed vision for the role of the preacher. Taken seriously, what our respondents said has vast implications for how we understand the preaching task itself. To be sure, these insights do not raise issues that are utterly new to the field of preaching. Instead, they suggest that, when cultural frames and cross-cultural aims play a central role, this naturally shifts the relative weights of what the preaching event will emphasize. Across the diverse settings of our interviewees, we discerned a pattern of four broad ways that preaching is now being configured, a stream of intertwined actions that preaching sets out to do.

To Partner

As important as we all know the preacher's role to be, it became abundantly clear through our interviews that effective cross-cultural preaching is a collaborative enterprise. The preacher surely sets the sermon in motion, but even the best homiletical intention falls flat unless the community of listeners becomes a partner in what is proclaimed. This community ultimately sets the terms by which the preaching has its significance. To be sure, this corresponds to a major shift in homiletics scholarship itself that began three decades ago and is continuing today, a shift toward so-called "listener-centered" preaching. What our research showed, however, was that our respondents did not treat this as an interesting theory but as a lived reality requiring specific strategies.

As we have seen throughout this book, this partnership is most directly evidenced *during* the preaching event itself. Overt verbal or bodily interaction has long been the practice with certain ethnic groups or religious traditions. In other cross-cultural settings, however, we learned how sermons can evoke a very strong response even though no obvious reactions are apparent. The key insight in all these cases is that in order for cross-cultural preaching to engage hearers deeply, it must presume mutuality in how meaning is constructed, regardless of how that mutuality might be expressed during the sermon. The reception of the sermon is easily as important to effectiveness as what the preacher intends, an insight that turns on its head what has often been taught about preaching.

Beyond the sermon itself, the partnership that typifies cross-cultural preaching has two other moments. In order for any collaboration to occur at all during the preaching event, there is always an intentional effort to build collaboration *beforehand*. Preachers work to invite those from diverse cultural backgrounds into the process of sermon preparation, such as studying biblical texts, exploring useful images, and so forth. At a symbolic level alone, involving unfamiliar or marginalized cultural groups in this way confers honor, treating their lives as a gift to the entire congregation. Their presence also serves a critical purpose, exposing the hidden biases and values that might keep the sermon from reaching more kinds of listeners. Still further, the resulting collaborative conversation gives the preacher access to cultural perspectives and grammars by which the preaching will be enriched and diversified. As those new perceptions and resources are woven into the sermon, the entire congregation is enhanced as well. Clearly, this kind of partnership runs counter to and takes greater effort than isolated forms of preparation, something that again changes how we think about the preaching task.

The partnership of preaching is not finished, however, without one final move. This is the mutual work that occurs *afterward,* when the sermon itself is finished. Collaborative preaching knows that the real test of its own effectiveness must extend beyond the final "Amen." In some congregations, post-sermon discussions provide an opportunity for raising questions and sharing further responses. Such discussions are decidedly not about evaluating the sermon or the preacher. Instead, they allow for alternative voices to be heard and valued and become a space for exploring the intersection between the preaching and daily life. This larger trajectory of partnership naturally leads back to collaborative possibilities for preparing upcoming sermons. Moreover, it can also promote a bond between groups that are otherwise culturally disparate, an outcome that moves into the next way that preaching is being understood anew.

To Connect

We have always expected that good preaching will connect the life of the hearer with the God revealed in scripture. Cross-cultural preaching takes that effort to connect a few steps further. For example, it tries to ensure that this fundamental revelatory connection is not subverted by cultural additions or distortions. This is why the partnership mentioned above is so important, serving as a safeguard against whatever may prevent such connections. Beyond this, however, our respondents conceived of preaching as also trying to connect the hearers with one another, lending a significant social and ecclesial purpose to the preaching event.

During our interviews, the topic of connections often took the conversation in directions seemingly unrelated to preaching. Only later did we realize why this happened. If preaching was ever to succeed at connecting, our respondents had to give prior attention to congregational *hospitality*. Pastors realized this had a direct bearing upon preaching, especially for visitors from diverse backgrounds who would surely face cultural differences. Long before the sermon began, these visitors would have to cross boundaries simply in meeting the existing members. Attention to hospitality thus demanded intentional and sometimes difficult work. One pastor spoke of it in terms of sacrifice.

> What it requires, I think, is a new ethic on the part of a congregation, and the ethic needs to be "I'm willing to forgo always being satisfied, for the sake of the community. The community is more important than me having the preaching, the worship, and the music always the way I want it." When that happens, I think, we have an opportunity for a new community, a unity growing out of diversity. But as long as we hold onto the idea that "it needs to satisfy me and me first—this is my church," I think that's going to be a very, very difficult time.

Put another way, the hospitality that enables preaching to connect calls for a spirit of generosity. Such generosity is shown not only in welcoming the newcomer but also throughout the congregational system. While this may again seem unrelated to the focus of this book, we repeatedly heard that preaching can build connections only when it is embedded in other similarly committed congregational practices. This is why, when talking about preaching, we were so frequently told instead about strategies for drawing underrepresented groups into key roles, as when the pastor of a Korean congregation referred to reaching out to new Chinese attendees. "The leadership of the church needs to immediately reflect the new people. You must incorporate them into the service. Chinese who come here, who can speak English, immediately become liturgists, or are encouraged to go right into the choir. You need to deal with the whole system, not just preaching." Such strategies provide a basis upon which preaching can build and expand. Hospitality is therefore integral to a new vision for preaching by enabling its work of connecting.

Turning more directly to the sermon itself, cross-cultural preaching seeks to connect by emphasizing especially what is *shared* between the hearers. There is something of a paradox in this. On the one hand, our respondents used culturally specific sermonic materials (stories, images, and so forth) to appeal to certain hearers, while on the other hand knowing that such materials would risk excluding other hearers. There was no general, generic option that reached all listeners equally. Instead, these preachers were skillful at exploring specific materials and perspectives for the deeper commonalities they revealed about all those who gathered. One preacher with over a dozen nationalities in attendance on any given

Sunday remarked: "Preaching has to be inclusive. You have to find something that resonates with everyone there. What you do is you look for the common ground. What are the feelings? What are those emotions? What are those stories that everybody can resonate with?" Note that these shared places of connection were at an affective and experiential level. Differences were not to be ignored but instead placed in a larger perspective. Another preacher said: "I am aware of the differences, but I try to expose them as challenges to find common ground. In my own spiritual walk, God has shown me more about the connections between things than the disconnections. That's what's working for me out in this community. That's what I view my call as—to know the differences but to stress the similarities." All of us know what it is to hunger or thirst, to grieve or rejoice, to despair or hope, even though these may be expressed quite differently due to our ethnicity, class, beliefs, and so forth. Nor are these commonalities unimportant, since human indifference to these shared realities has been the source of untold suffering throughout the world. It should come as no surprise, then, that scripture is able to speak across cultures precisely because it addresses these shared aspects of our lives. In forging connections, preaching therefore takes on a serious new task of showing that we have more in common with our culturally diverse neighbors than not, sharing both a deep human wound and a deep human longing for restoration.

Related to this, our interviews clarified that one other way preaching can connect is through *celebration*. Fundamental to this is the conviction that our truest bond is not one we make among ourselves but the one God creates with us. There is no more substantial or relevant connection between us than the life we first receive through Jesus Christ. Trusting in this, effective cross-cultural preaching culminates in a move of joy: the confident freedom to face whatever befalls us knowing that the source of life is God alone. Such joy is enacted in unique cultural forms, of course, and employing these within the sermon eventually becomes ordinary rather than exceptional. By voicing such celebration, as well as by building on hospitality and expressing what we share, preaching becomes a way to connect. Attentive to culture, preaching is changing to become more of a sign of unity and wholeness for the sake of the church, a development that leads us into another shift in the nature of preaching.

To Signal

In a simple communication model of preaching, the sermon is like any other message being transmitted from sender to receiver. The accuracy of the transmission process is tested against whether the message has been received more or less intact. This is usually judged in terms of the sermon's content, whether the received meaning matches what the preacher intended. Despite the limitations of this model it continues to be a useful shorthand, and throughout this book we have referred to aspects of effective cross-cultural preaching in just this manner. Even so, it is significant that our interviewees were also operating implicitly with another view of preaching, a semiotic model. Such a model focuses on what the entire preaching task symbolizes and enacts. Preaching is judged less as a content or meaning than as a sign, something that bears the reality to which it points.

One way preaching signifies is through its emphasis on particular *forms*. Traditionally, preaching has been deeply entrenched in forms essentially derived from the prophetic oracle. That is, the sermon is a divine word of weal or woe uttered through a chosen agent to a specific community. By contrast, we have often seen in this book a preference for narrative forms of preaching that create an alternative reality into which the hearer is drawn. These narratives work rather indirectly to rebuild a people and connect them to a larger story that is valued and claimed by God. In addition to narrative forms, our respondents often used expressive forms in their preaching, such as lament and praise. These forms are no mere emotional ornaments but instead validate that every portion of our lives can be honestly brought before God and will be met by divine mercy. When preachers attend to culture and thus explore these forms, the sermon itself becomes more than just a content to be absorbed. By its very form, preaching signals an encounter with God in which memory is reconstructed, experiences are affirmed, and dignity is conferred.

Another way preaching signifies is in its role as a *gift*, a bearer of the very graciousness it designates. It is worth remembering that no one compelled our respondents to preach as they did. Once they recognized the challenges within their settings, however, they embraced rather than avoided them. At heart, this was because they had already heard the lavishness of Christ and thus echoed this in their overall pastoral ministry. It only became natural, then, to treat the sermon as well suited to be similarly gracious. As a result, they voluntarily and eagerly adopted strategies that would enable others to hear this same gift of Christ as well.

It is important to clarify just how radical this concept of gift truly is. In ordinary life, a gift often carries with it an implicit debt. What is given demands some kind of response or expected return. By contrast, our respondents saw preaching as an utterly free offer that created no later obligation. This meant that conditions, manipulation, moralizing, and harangue had no place. Sermons were not driven by seeking change in the hearers or approval of the preacher, even though such outcomes were sometimes by-products. Unconstrained by utilitarian aims, preaching plainly signals the abundant offer of life known specifically in Christ. Because preaching re-presents that same Christ, its very approach is transformed. In humble and self-giving love, those we interviewed were taking the initiative to make risky claims, an approach that lent their preaching a new degree of freshness and vibrancy. By showing such a gift, moreover, preaching is able to create the kinds of connections between hearers that we mentioned earlier.

Related to this, one additional way preaching signifies is by indicating a horizon of *hope*. Our interviewees noted that deeper appreciation of cultural groups led in turn to greater awareness of division, hatred, abuse, and harm. Such awareness is why they were so concerned about the matters of hospitality mentioned earlier in this chapter, of course. Specifically in terms of preaching, however, many preachers said they now gave much greater attention to God's works of liberation and justice in society. Others added with surprise that eschatological themes had become increasingly relevant, not as cheap comfort but in order to show divine faithfulness. In all such cases, preaching plays a pivotal role in signifying hope itself. It declares first and foremost the ancient claim that God has made us a new people, rescuing us from sin, fear, and death. Next, it calls to mind God's lasting commitment to this promise, even and especially when life looks otherwise. Building on this claim and commitment, preaching then serves as a beacon, directing our lives toward the reality granted through Christ. For these reasons, concern for cultural diversity is moving the character of preaching beyond a merely personal focus to make it a broader sign of the hope we bear in Christ for all people and the whole creation.

To Witness

We would naturally expect effective cross-cultural preachers to reject the idea that a sermon is a private conversation intended solely for insiders. Through addressing cultural realities, preaching is regaining its outward impetus as a public declaration. Yet this shift should not be naively understood. It is common today to hear preaching referred to as a tool for witnessing to outsiders, attracting them to church for the sake of numerical growth. Those we interviewed, however, understood witnessing in a very different way. Indeed, their efforts to appeal broadly amid cultural diversity, even to the alienated and marginalized, were quite at odds with the niche marketing techniques of the so-called church growth movement. How, then, did our respondents actually think anew of preaching that serves to witness?

Above all, preaching is being seen as a witness to *God's mission*. We are perhaps more familiar with thinking of mission as something *we* do in obedient response to divine instruction. To speak of God's mission, however, reestablishes the ground of mission and how we enter into it. From the dawn of creation to its consummation, God's movement toward the world is for the sake of abundant life. God's mission confounds all of our rational schemes and respects none of our self-imposed limits. It is a divine generosity whose trajectory has a cosmic sweep. Into this mission the church is drawn, and to it alone the church gives witness, as opposed to boasting of its own programs, plans, or achievements. As a distinctive discourse of the church joined to God's mission, preaching fundamentally gives witness to God's boundless mercy and love. By its very nature, then, such preaching becomes cross-cultural in intent. Seeking to witness to what God has done and will do, preaching accepts no boundaries of human invention.

Connected with this, the witness of preaching occurs through the *faithful* who gather for worship. Although this appears to reintroduce an internal focus to the sermon, just the opposite is in fact the case. When our respondents noticed the cultural dimensions of their settings, they also realized the breadth of the world already being brought into worship. For all of our cultural particularities, each of us exists in a web of relationships with other people and cultures. In a very important sense, then, the church at worship is always a microcosm, a sign of and for the whole world. By highlighting the world of connections already present at worship, preaching can then proceed to empower the faithful to witness to God's mission in daily life. This corresponds with our earlier remarks about the emerging view of preaching as a partnership, one now focused on the task of witness. Instead of this task resting solely on the preacher's shoulders, however, it is borne now by all the faithful. Moreover, this reminds us again that preaching can be truly cross-cultural regardless of the personal cultural characteristics of those at worship.

A further way we can speak of this shift is to note that, by seeking to witness, preaching becomes increasingly *worldly*. Because God's mission is for the sake of the world and because the church joined to this mission embodies that world, preaching is itself more deeply open to the world, and in several senses. For the sake of this witness, scripture is now used in a more worldly way in preaching, examined for the social and cultural worlds it asserts, critiques, and suppresses. In a similar way, human lives and experiences are heard as potent new sources precisely because they offer a range of perspectives through which preaching can engage others more fully. Last but not least, worldly preaching is emerging as an accountable word, immersed in a dialogue with alternative witnesses and willingly facing correction and even rejection in the process. No longer standing apart from the world by being above or alongside it, preaching is now *in* the world as a serious witness to Christ, attending to the very substance of the cosmos for which Christ's life was given. This may be the single most important way that commitment to cultural diversity from the pulpit is transforming our view of preaching, centering it in the world in order to witness to the life of the world.

One Final Voice

During the course of our research, we became acquainted with a preacher whose experiences typify the focus of this book. Still in his first congregation, he had originally been called there to assist the venerable lead minister. When this colleague died only five years later, however, the mantle of authority suddenly became his. It was an awesome burden. Although the setting in which he now served was a mere sixty miles from where he had grown up, the two places were really worlds apart. A sleepy little village, his hometown was just like hundreds of others that dotted the rural hill country. By contrast, the church he served was in a bustling city on the coast, a major commercial and transportation center. It was a lively place where the whole world seemed to gather, a stunning diversity that this preacher found both appealing and daunting.

If the gap between big city and hometown seemed immense, how much more so was that between the urban residents and the folks back home. The preacher's family seemed stamped out of the same mold as its neighbors. Most were lifelong residents who knew each other's stories, shared a common heritage, and differed little in values or temperament. All of them were traditional and hard-working people just scraping to make ends meet. By comparison, the cosmopolitan residents among whom this preacher now served were a bundle of contrasts. As we learned more about them, we quickly realized that they vividly displayed a range of diversity that can barely be suggested through the four cultural frames developed in this book.

Most visible of these differences were those of class. Like many such cities, both opulence and squalor were easy to spot. The very neighborhood in which the church sat was wealthy and elite, but the preacher spent most of his days in the less desirable parts of town, areas crowded with ugly apartments and low-cost housing. For reasons no one could explain, these lower-class, poorly educated residents comprised the majority of his congregation. As a result, he entered their world and heard their stories of menial work, harsh treatment, and hopes for tomorrow. He also was privy to the disgust expressed by his few well-to-do members who could barely contain their contempt for those on the bottom rungs of society. He had even felt the sting of their arrogance himself, the little snubs and put-downs intended to say that he was not quite good enough.

Overlapping these realities were ethnic distinctions. Not as pronounced as class issues, ethnicity still played a role by forcing people into one of two camps. On the one hand were those who quietly prided themselves for holding true to their national roots as descendents of the pioneers who originally settled the region long ago. On the other hand were the relative newcomers who had moved to the city from the south, ridiculed as a mongrel group with strange ways and a crude country accent. Although ethnic tensions between the two factions rarely came out in the open, underlying suspicion kept them completely at arm's length. Each group wanted as little to do with the other as possible, and so they lived instead in two separate and insulated ethnic worlds.

The composition of the city was rapidly changing, however, as immigrants brought a new sense of cultural displacement. Some were victims of an economic slump in the surrounding rural areas, people who moved from country to city simply to find work. Others were political refugees from various wars and purges overseas, people who escaped with the resources they could carry and were now hoping to start over. As a result of these sudden shifts to the population, even a few of the old guard began to feel alienated as well. They longed for the good old days when the economy was booming and no one feared violence in the streets. This alienation had led some of them even to move away, becoming absentee landlords who only visited on rare occasions. All told, the many forms of displacement seemed to be tearing the city's social fabric apart.

Yet nothing was a more threatening cultural challenge for this preacher than that of beliefs. In such a city, he had expected to find numerous religious alternatives, from obscure offshoot sects to well-known faith traditions from around the world. Eventually, he had also begun to recognize a peculiar local form of patriotism that seemed to be a civil religion all of its own. Nothing, however, had prepared him for the open hostility dished out by fellow Christians who worshiped in a church almost directly across the street from his own. These were relentless conservatives, a force to be reckoned with because theirs was in fact the predominant piety in this city. Still new to his role, this preacher therefore faced the unenviable task of leading a congregation that these neighboring believers did not even regard as truly Christian.

If this situation sounds like a potent cultural tempest in which to minister, it was. If it sounds like the cross-cultural challenge we must learn to address through our preaching, it is. If it sounds like a place you might actually have seen, however, then think again. Although this preacher was beset by an array of cultural challenges surely as great as any today, he actually faced them long ago and far away. In fact, his pastoral service began near the end of the fourth century, his congregation was located in the Roman colony of Hippo Regius (on the coast of modern-day Algeria), and his name was Aurelius Augustinus—better known today as St. Augustine.

In his thirty-four years as bishop of Hippo, Augustine preached twice per week, not including special festivals and commemorations. Although only about a hundred and fifty sermons of undisputed authorship survive from his preaching there, they give a glimpse of someone who knew his cultural scene intimately and addressed it fearlessly. The class structures that pitted plebeians and slaves against patricians, the ethnic coexistence of Italian colonists with those of Punic descent, the sense of displacement known both by migrating farmers and refugees from Vandal attacks, and the religious conflicts between Donatists and Catholics—all these and more were reflected in his sermons. Were these challenges not enough, Augustine also lived in a society whose daily violence causes us to shudder.

This was the setting Augustine engaged not only in sermons but also in a treatise about how to preach. Soon after his arrival in Hippo, he began to compose what is arguably the first complete text on Christian preaching, *On Christian Doctrine*. The few preachers who read it anymore typically focus only on its final section, a handbook on how to organize, compose, and deliver sermons. We rarely stop to consider that it emerged not as a cool, scholarly reflection but in response to the heated cross-cultural challenges that Augustine regularly faced as a North African bishop. Worse still, we end up overlooking the first three-fourths of *On Christian Doctrine,* which is actually devoted to *preparation* for preaching, especially how we ought to interpret scripture. Amid the cultural storms and stresses in which he preached, Augustine spent most of his energy showing how to read a book rather than how to appeal to crowds. It is worthwhile to ask why.

Augustine's interpretive approach is based on clarifying just what kind of thing scripture is. Like everything else in creation, scripture has been given by God in order to be used rather than enjoyed. Only God may be enjoyed for God's own sake. Created things, by contrast, are to be used so that they lead to God and thus true enjoyment. The proper way to use scripture so that it leads to God rests in a simple key: love. "The sum of all we have said since we began to speak of things thus comes to this, that the fulfillment and the end of the law and of all the sacred scriptures is love" [I.35.39]. To be sure, Augustine knew the complexities of scriptural language that holds multiple levels of meaning, a matter he treated in his theory of signs. Even so, love remains the central principle that orients how scripture is to be read so that it leads to God and thus enjoyment of the divine.

What is striking in light of Augustine's particular setting is that this love is never abstract. It takes concrete form in human society and is known by a specific test. He continues, "Whoever, therefore, supposes to understand the divine scriptures or any part of them so that it does not build up the double love of God and of the neighbor does not understand it at all" [I.36.40]. We should pause to consider the depth of this simple remark. Scripture, properly used, leads to enjoyment of God. Yet the test for properly using scripture toward this end is whether it contributes to love of God *and the neighbor.*

Specific to the larger purpose of *On Christian Doctrine,* therefore, the test for good preaching is similar: whether the scripture is proclaimed in a way that leads to love, concretely seen in love of the neighbor. In the divided, uncertain, and often hostile cultural setting in which Augustine lived, this was no petty claim. Preaching truly served Christ to the degree that it evoked love between Donatists and Catholics, patricians and slaves, Italians and Punics, and all the other culturally diverse neighbors in Hippo. Anything else would be a misuse of scripture, because anything else would lead away from God.

We are unfamiliar and perhaps uncomfortable with having so much riding on our preaching. We prefer to be selective about cross-cultural efforts, waiting for opportunities that are easy, rational, and safe. Augustine, however, has a markedly counter-cultural vision. In a sermon preached near the close of the fourth century, Augustine asked his hearers what they expected from preaching. Answering his own question, he said: "What is learned is how to live a good life; and how to live a good life is learned to enable you to live forever. . . . There you are, that's what's learned in the house of discipline: to love God, to love your neighbor; God as God, your neighbor as yourself." [*Sermon* 399.1,3]*

If preaching is truly to lead us to God, then it calls for a particular sort of love, a love tested in the crucible of daily life. The way we began this book is therefore the way we end it: cross-cultural preaching is finally driven by nothing other than love of neighbor.

*Saint Augustine: On Christian Doctrine, trans. D. W. Robertson Jr. (New York: Macmillan Publishing Co., 1958); John E. Rotelle, ed. *Sermons (341–400) on Various Subjects,* in *The Works of Saint Augustine: A Translation for the 21st Century,* vol. 3, trans. Edmund Hill (Hyde Park, N.Y.: New City Press, 1995).

Suggested Readings

This selective list of readings is provided for those who wish to explore more deeply the background literature that has informed this book. These texts do not discuss preaching per se, but instead address the theoretical issues that bear upon cross-cultural preaching. Except for the last section, these recommendations are grouped under headings that correspond to the four frames used in this book.

Ethnicity

Gilroy, Paul. *Against Race: Imagining Political Culture beyond the Color Line.* Cambridge, Mass.: The Belknap Press, 2000.

Matsuoka, Fumitaka. *The Color of Faith: Building Community in a Multiracial Society.* Cleveland: United Church Press, 1998.

Thankdeka. *Learning to Be White: Money, Race and God in America.* New York: Continuum, 2000.

West, Cornel. *Race Matters.* New York: Vintage Books, 1994.

Class

Bloomquist, Karen L. *The Dream Betrayed: Religious Challenge of the Working Class.* Minneapolis: Fortress Press, 1990.

Gibson-Graham, J. K., Stephen A. Resnick, and Richard D. Wolff, eds. *Class and Its Others.* Foreword by Amitava Kuvar. Minneapolis: University of Minnesota Press, 2000.

Sample, Tex. *Blue-Collar Ministry: Facing Economic and Social Realities of Working People.* Valley Forge: Judson Press, 1984.

Sennett, Richard, and Jonathan Cobb. *The Hidden Injuries of Class.* New York: W. W. Norton and Company, 1972.

Displacement

Altman, Irwin, and Setha M. Low. *Place Attachment.* Human Behavior and Environment Series, vol. 12. New York: Plenum Publishing Corp., 1992.

Boym, Svetlana. *The Future of Nostalgia.* New York: Basic Books, 2001. See especially part 1.

Leach, William. *Country of Exiles: The Destruction of Place in American Life.* New York: Pantheon Books, 1999.

Portes, Alejandro, and Rúben G. Rumbaut. *Immigrant America: A Portrait.* 2d ed. Berkeley: University of California Press, 1996.

Beliefs

Baumann, Gerd. *The Multicultural Riddle: Rethinking National, Ethnic, and Religious Identities.* New York: Routledge, 1999.

Cobb, John B., Jr. *Transforming Christianity and the World: A Way beyond Absolutism and Relativism.* Edited and introduced by Paul F. Knitter. Maryknoll, N.Y.: Orbis Books, 1999.

Heim, S. Mark. *Salvations: Truth and Difference in Religion.* Maryknoll, N.Y.: Orbis Books, 1995.

Nazir-Ali, Michael. *Citizens and Exiles: Christian Faith in a Plural World.* Cleveland: United Church Press, 1998.

Panikkar, Raimon. *The Intrareligious Dialogue.* Rev. ed. New York: Paulist Press, 1999.

Communication

Gudykunst, William B., and Young Yun Kim. *Communicating with Strangers: An Approach to Intercultural Communication.* 2d ed. New York: McGraw Hill, Inc., 1992.

Ong, Walter J. *Orality and Literacy: The Technologizing of the Word.* Edited by Terence Hawkes. New Accents series. New York: Routledge, 1982.

Samovar, Larry A., and Richard E. Porter. *Communication between Cultures.* Belmont, Calif.: Wadsworth Publishing Co., 1991.

Sikkema, Mildred, and Agnes Niyekawa. *Design for Cross-Cultural Learning.* Yarmouth, Md.: Intercultural Press, Inc., 1987.

Tanner, Kathryn. *Theories of Culture: A New Agenda for Theology.* Guides to Theological Inquiry series. Minneapolis: Fortress Press, 1997.

Wiseman, Richard L. *Intercultural Communication Theory.* International and Intercultural Communication Annual Series, vol. 19. Thousand Oaks, Calif.: Sage Publications, Inc., 1995.